CHRISTIANITY AND PROCESS THOUGHT

Christianity and Process Thought

Spirituality for a Changing World

Joseph A. Bracken, S. J.

TEMPLETON FOUNDATION PRESS

PHILADELPHIA AND LONDON

Templeton Foundation Press
300 Conshohocken State Road, Suite 670
West Conshohocken, PA 19428
www.templetonpress.org

Templeton Foundation Press helps intellectual leaders and others learn about science research on aspects of realities, invisible and intangible. Spiritual realities include unlimited love, accelerating creativity, worship, and the benefits of purpose in persons and in the cosmos.

Library of Congress Cataloging-in-Publication Data
Bracken, Joseph A.
  Christianity and process thought : spirituality for a changing world
/ Joseph A. Bracken.
    p. cm.
  ISBN-13: 978-1-932031-98-0 (pbk. : alk. paper)
  ISBN-10: 1-932031-98-7 (pbk. : alk. paper) 1. Philosophical theology. 2. Process theology. 3. Spirituality. I. Title.
  BT55.B73 2006
  230'.046—dc22
                                                          2005026729

Printed in the United States of America

06 07 08 09 10   10 9 8 7 6 5 4 3 2 1

To the memory of Jim Hoff, S. J.
who mercilessly teased me about process theology
but who now knows better (one way or another),
this book is affectionately dedicated.

Contents

Foreword

FOR CENTURIES Christian spirituality was built on the assumption that perfection means changelessness. Not only God but also the heavens were thought to be essentially immutable. Only on Earth, where imperfection is so obvious, did things move, and their movement was the emblem of their imperfection. Although the heavens as a whole swept in wide circles around the Earth, it was unthinkable that the blemish of novelty could ever show up in the celestial spheres. Perfection meant permanence, the absence of change and becoming. As the unfading lights from above shone down on the world, they invited people to lift up their hearts to the immutable divine goodness transparent in them.

It is important to realize how intricately religious awareness has been woven into this cosmology of fixity. To a great extent it still is. We have not yet fully worked our way through the spiritual trauma that set in when Copernicus, Brahe, Kepler, Galileo—and later Einstein and Hubble—exposed the super-lunary world as itself mobile and unfinished. It has not made spirituality less challenging that Charles Darwin placed the realm of life in a continuous stream of becoming and that present-day microphysics thrusts us even more decisively into a world in which movement rather than fixity is the dominant feature. But in such a fluid world what happens to our irrepressible longing for perfection?

The idea that perfection means absolute immutability still

lives on. Who can deny that the religious sensibilities of most people in the world remain most at home in a prescientific understanding of the universe? Theology has moved only slowly and often reluctantly away from the ancient cosmological assumptions in which it came to birth. And even where notional awareness has conceded the correctness of an evolutionary worldview, Christian spirituality still remains emotionally fastened to the pillar of permanence stamped into our consciousness long before the coming of modern science.

People of all times and places, of course, need something toward which to direct their aspirations for perfection, and this is true no less today than ever. But it is hardly a credit to contemporary theology that the spiritual instincts of most people, including many of the scientifically educated, still seem so out of sync with our new understanding of nature. Joseph Bracken, however, is one of a relative minority of contemporary theologians who have taken with full seriousness the task of aligning spiritual longing and religious thought with what we now know to be true about the natural world. He has spent much of his distinguished academic career working out a sophisticated conceptual framework that can bring together science and Christian doctrine coherently.

Professor Bracken began to realize quite early, however, that such a synthesis cannot be accomplished as long as the conceptual tools available to theological reflection are limited to those provided by ancient and medieval thinkers, resourceful as these may otherwise be. What contemporary theology needs, since it still cannot get by without the help of philosophy, is a system of concepts that takes science, religion, and all other modes of experience into full account. Happily the philosophy of Alfred North Whitehead provides at least much of the apparatus to build such a system.

Developing his theology in the context of Whiteheadian process thought, the author of this timely book has been able to link science and its disclosure of a world-in-motion with the aspiration to perfection that has always been central to human spiritual existence. Substituting process for permanence, emphasizing the fact of subjectivity instead of the monotony of materialist mechanism, and acknowledging the primacy of dynamic relationality in place of fixed substantiality, he is able to show that spiritual longing is not taken away but only enlivened.

Along with the Bible and Christian tradition, Whitehead's philosophy—which Bracken is not loath to criticize when necessary—provides the basis here for a Christian spirituality that can face head-on the world revealed by science without diminishing the importance and indispensability of religious faith. The unique contribution of the following pages is to make the spiritual implications of this grand synthesis available to many levels of readership in a clear and accessible manner.

John F. Haught
Georgetown University

Acknowledgments

SEVERAL PEOPLE assisted me in converting Whitehead's insights and the technical terms of his philosophy into more readable commonsense language. In particular, I would like to acknowledge the help of Sr. Nancy Vollman, O.S.U (a well-known spiritual director in the Cincinnati archdiocese), Rev. Terry Smith (former pastor at St. Columban Parish in Loveland, Ohio, where I work on weekends), and Rev. Gene Carmichael, S.J. (fellow Jesuit community member at Xavier University in Cincinnati). All three kept prodding me to write in a more conversational (as opposed to a formal academic) style. Likewise, I am grateful for the initial encouragement of Dr. Billy Grassie of the Metanexus Institute in Philadelphia and Dr. Tom Oord of Northwest Nazarene University in Nampa, Idaho, to publish my manuscript with the Templeton Foundation Press. Finally, I am grateful to Laura Barrett and her staff at the Press for facilitating its rapid publication.

Introduction

For MANY YEARS I have used the philosophy of Alfred North Whitehead for my teaching and writing in both philosophy and theology. Whitehead was a distinguished mathematician and theoretical physicist who taught at Trinity College, Cambridge University, in England, and then at University College, London, in the early twentieth century before taking a newly created position at Harvard University in the United States in 1924. At Harvard he focused his attention on philosophy—above all, on cosmology or the principles underlying change or evolution in the world of nature. Until his death in 1947, Whitehead published many works in philosophy, including *Process and Reality: An Essay in Cosmology* (1929), the revised version of his celebrated Gifford Lectures in Scotland in 1927–1928. His highly original approach to reality unquestionably took many people by surprise. Professional philosophers in England and the United States were by and large somewhat slow to follow his lead, but many theologians saw in Whitehead's philosophy the basis for a new understanding of the God-world relationship.

Speaking for myself, I can testify that his process-oriented approach to reality immediately fired my imagination to think through all over again my basic Christian beliefs about God and our relationship to God, both as individuals and as a worshiping community. Furthermore, in my preaching on Sundays in various parishes I found myself instinctively resorting to key ideas out of Whitehead's philosophy, albeit in somewhat simplified form, so as to illuminate Scripture passages of the day. To my pleasant surprise, I often received highly favorable comments from parishioners. But, in point of fact, I should not have been surprised, for Whitehead's thought is in many ways better attuned to the conventional understanding of Holy Scripture than the philosophy and theology of Thomas Aquinas, the Dominican monk whose thought has been the benchmark for Roman Catholic thought since the thirteenth century. Where Aquinas emphasized God's transcendent reality as Creator of heaven and earth, Whitehead proposes that God is necessarily involved in an ongoing, ever-changing relationship with creatures. Just as pictured on the pages of sacred Scripture, Whitehead's God responds with feelings of joy or sadness to what is happening in the world. God thus shares in our world in a way that is logically impossible for the somewhat distant, unchanging God of traditional Thomistic philosophy and theology.

Yet, given this obvious attractiveness of Whitehead's thought for the interpretation of sacred Scripture and the explanation of basic Christian beliefs, it has been for me somewhat disappointing to note over the years the relatively cool reception given to process-oriented philosophy and theology by fellow Christians, most notably by Roman Catholic colleagues in philosophy and theology. In some measure, this is surely due to the preeminence of Bernard Lonergan, Karl Rahner, and Urs von Balthasar in Roman Catholic systematic theology. The richness of their thought has sustained most Roman Catholic theologians for the past half-century. Likewise, one can point to the technical character of Whitehead's basic concepts—hence, the difficulty in coming to terms with a totally new approach to reality—as reason enough for Roman Catholics as well as many mainstream Protestant theologians to postpone or simply put off reading works in process theology even though the process image of God as being in ongoing communication with the world of creation is otherwise so attractive.

A deeper reason for this unresponsiveness to the project of process theology, however, in my judgment lies elsewhere. Process theology is unhappily linked in the minds of many Roman Catholics and mainstream Protestants with a tendency to eliminate or explain away some of their most cherished Christian beliefs, even as it offers new insight into still other beliefs, as noted above. For example, doctrines such as *creatio ex nihilo* (creation out of nothing), with its emphasis on God's free self-gift in the act of creation, and classical eschatology (the doctrine of the "four last things": death, judgment, heaven, and hell) with its promise of eternal life not only for human beings but for all of material creation, have been either set aside or significantly underplayed by the disciples of Whitehead in their sustained focus on life here and now in a rapidly changing world. Too little effort, as I see it, has been expended in somehow adjusting Whitehead's philosophical categories to accommodate those same traditional Christian beliefs. The deeper issue, therefore, for many Roman Catholics and mainstream Protestants seems to be whether one ultimately puts one's faith in Whitehead's metaphysical scheme or in the established belief system of one's church.

Ideally, the two should enrich one another. Just as Aquinas reconceived the philosophy of Aristotle so as to accommodate basic Christian beliefs about God and the world and in the process came up with some new philosophical insights into the nature of reality, so Whitehead's process-relational metaphysics should both enrich traditional Christian theology and be enriched by it. Yet this convergence of viewpoints is still not finished. I myself have worked for many years at such a revision of Whitehead's metaphysics so as to accommodate the basic Christian beliefs mentioned above. Over time I have developed a new understanding of the God-world relationship in which all creatures come forth from the triune God and return to God as members of an all-embracing cosmic community. Strong emphasis is thus laid on the freedom of the three divine persons to create and the corresponding freedom of creatures to respond to what Whitehead calls divine "initial aims." Out of this prolonged comparison of Whitehead's metaphysics and basic Christian beliefs, moreover, has come the conviction on my part that initial inconsistencies in point of view between Whitehead's philosophy and basic Christian beliefs can over time be harmonized, to the ultimate advantage of both faith and reason.

Yet friends have also reminded me that I cannot present these new insights into the creative link between Whitehead's philosophy and classical Christian theology in the formal language of process-relational metaphysics and expect most of them to follow my line of thought. Accommodation must be somehow made to their more conventional understanding of reality until the Whiteheadian scheme of things begins to sink in. The real challenge, of course, is not thereby to lose the originality of Whitehead's metaphysical vision even as one tries to explain it in more commonsense language. Here I will certainly do my best, but I ask the reader to be patient if initially some of Whitehead's basic concepts seem rather strange, even bizarre. From my own experience I can say that, if one perseveres in the effort at comprehension, the deeper logic of this approach to reality will gradually become clear. This in turn sparks the imagination, and one finds oneself unexpectedly hooked on Whitehead. He was undoubtedly one of the most original thinkers of the twentieth century, someone well worth the extra effort to read and understand.

Before concluding, I wish to add one more introductory remark. Since the doctrine of the Trinity figures prominently in my approach to the God-world relationship, I face a modest dilemma in deciding upon appropriate names or titles for the divine persons. The traditional names of "Father," "Son," and "Holy Spirit" have been rightly called into question by Elizabeth Johnson and other Christian feminists, for these names or titles implicitly carry forward and promote a form of patriarchy within Christianity that many contemporary men and women with good reason repudiate.[1] But they still are the names most widely used by Christians both in public worship and in academic discourse, albeit with some uneasiness since there is as yet no commonly agreed-upon new set of names or titles. Paradoxically, however, if one consciously uses Whitehead's new categories and modes of thought for thinking about the God-world relationship, the dilemma about the use of the divine names seems to disappear. For example, as a Whiteheadian, I find myself normally thinking in nonsexist terms about the three divine persons. Each divine person is to be understood not as male or female but simply as a subject of experience with an infinite or totally unlimited field of activity proper to its own form of existence. There are no sexist overtones here since, as we will see below, subjects of experience, or what Whitehead calls "actual occasions," are likewise the building blocks or ultimate constituents of everything that exists, even of inanimate things (atoms, molecules, etc.). Hence, a Whiteheadian actual occasion or subject of experience is by definition sexually neutral. One simply does not ask whether it is male or female since it could be either or neither in any given case.

In any event, as a practical measure here and now in writing this book, I put the traditional divine names in quotation marks the first time that they are used in any given chapter so as to indicate their nonliteral, purely metaphorical usage. After that, simply as a matter of convenience I use Father, Son, and Holy Spirit as the conventional terms for the three divine persons without further qualification. At the same time, I try to speak of the divine persons in the plural and refer to them as "they" wherever possible. In this way I generally avoid use of the pronoun "he" or "his" with reference to the divine persons.

CHRISTIANITY AND PROCESS THOUGHT

◀•▶

CHAPTER 1

"In Whom We Live and Move and Have Our Being" (Acts 17:28)

I F SOMEONE WERE TO ASK "Where is God?" how would you respond? Would you raise your finger in the air and point to the sky, saying "Up there!" After all, didn't Jesus ascend into heaven in front of his astonished disciples (Acts 1:9)? Or would you turn the finger on yourself, point to your heart, and say, "In here!" For, didn't Jesus also say: "Whoever loves me will keep my word, and my Father will love him, and we will come to him and make our dwelling with him" (John 14:23)? Or perhaps as a third alternative, one might say, "God is everywhere." But there is risk in all three answers. If God is limited to being either in heaven above or in the human heart here below, then how can God truly be God, Creator of heaven and earth and ruler of all things in this world? But, on the contrary, if God is everywhere, then equivalently God is nowhere. God does not exist. "God" is just the name for a childish fantasy carried over uncritically into adulthood.

These questions remind us of how important it is to have a model or symbolic representation of how God and the world relate to one another. Every such model, of course, is in one way or another deficient since we cannot shrink down to human proportions what infinitely exceeds our power to comprehend. But without some implicit model of the God-world relationship at work in our minds and hearts, the reality of God tends to disappear or be ignored as we focus simply on the world in front of us. Furthermore, as I explain below, the choice of a model is not purely arbitrary. There are practical consequences for us in virtue of the model we consciously or unconsciously choose to work with.

Perhaps the best traditional model for the God-world relationship was provided by the great medieval theologian Thomas Aquinas. Answering the question whether God is present in the world, Aquinas replies that God is present in every creature so as to keep it in existence.[1] Since God is Pure Being, the creature only exists in virtue of God's ongoing creative activity in its regard. But, Aquinas adds, while God is everywhere, God does not take up any space. Rather, God spiritually coexists with physical bodies as the invisible cause of their existence and activity.[2] God is thus everywhere in creation as the cause of the existence and activity of creatures, in virtue of God's knowledge and love of creatures, and through God's all-encompassing power.[3]

This is a marvelously concise description of God's relation to the world of creation, and it has certainly stood the test of time for most Christians. But it still has its limitations. While God is evidently present and active in the world, the world as the ongoing effect of God's creative activity still exists apart from or outside of God as its Creator or transcendent First Cause. Yet St. Paul says, in God "we live and move and have our being" (Acts 17:28). Perhaps Paul was carried away by his own rhetoric on this occasion when talking to philosophers in the Agora at Athens. But there still seems to be a logical problem in saying at one and the same time that God is infinite, without limitations, and that creation exists apart from God or outside of God. If creation is somehow outside of God, is God still truly infinite, without any limitations?

Still another deficiency of Aquinas's model for the God-world relationship has to do with our relation to God as God's creatures. If all that we are and have is simply the effect of God's ongoing creative activity in our regard, are we in any way free to be ourselves, to act independently of God and God's will for us at this moment? Most of us believe that the three divine persons empower us to make our own decisions; they do not overpower us by a unilateral exercise of divine power. But, if that is indeed the case, how is that compatible with Aquinas's approach in which everything exists only because God makes it happen? How can we be genuinely free to make our own decisions and still be totally dependent on God for our very being from moment to moment?

Partly for these reasons, some contemporary theologians have tested out other models for the God-world relationship. One of these theologians is Sallie McFague in her book *Models of God*.[4] She endorses the model of God as the "Soul" of the universe and the universe as the "body" of God. She is careful to say, of course, that this model of the God-world relationship is not to be taken literally.[5] Models of the God-world relationship should be taken seriously but certainly not literally.[6] But even so, is her model any better or even as good as that of Aquinas? Thinking of God as the "Soul" of the universe and the world as the "body" of God seems to jeopardize the independence of God from the world and the independence of the world from God. If soul and body are inseparable within human beings, what does that say about our relation to God and God's relation to us? Her theory, in other words, borders on pantheism, the identification of God with the world and vice versa, something condemned by the church.

McFague is aware of this danger. But what she likes about the model is the way in which it presents God as knowing the world directly and immediately, just as we know our own bodies directly and immediately: "God relates sympathetically to the world, just as we relate sympathetically to our bodies."[7] We cannot ignore what goes on in our bodies; God cannot ignore what happens in the world, above all, when pain and suffering are involved. Thus, as she sees it, God does not overcome evil in the world by divine decree. Rather, God suffers with creatures in their pain and suffering. With loving concern God assists them to work through the pain and suffering and achieve something worthwhile in the end.[8]

Yet the limitations of her model still remain. God seems to be much too dependent on creation within this model. McFague suggests that if this world were blown up or otherwise destroyed, then God would establish a relation with still another world.[9] But, at least for most Christians, this still raises the question of God's freedom to create or not to create. If God can't be without some world, even if not necessarily our world, does God create out of love, a desire to share the divine life with creatures, or out of necessity simply to be God? McFague has a clever response: "We are not submerged parts of the body of God but relate to God as to another Thou."[10] Likewise we encounter the physical world around us "as the body of God where God is present to us always in all times and in all places."[11] Thus thinking of God, the world, and one another in terms of ongoing I-Thou relationships, we are encouraged to take more responsibility for the world in which we live, a world that is endangered by the possibility of nuclear war and ecological disaster.[12]

I could not agree with McFague more on this point, but I also believe that her soul/body metaphor for the God-world relationship lacks credibility, at least in the way she presents it. For example, McFague is surely correct in saying that we human beings should have an interpersonal relationship with

God our Creator. Likewise, we should strive for better inter-personal relationship with the people we meet every day. But what about the world of Nature? Isn't it pure sentimentality to refer to plants and animals as Thou? Maybe we can have such an interpersonal relationship with our household pet, but surely not with most other animals and still less with trees, bushes, and other forms of plant life. So many of these animals and plants we routinely kill or harvest in order to feed ourselves. Finally, since most of the world is made up of inanimate things, atoms and molecules in intricate combination, isn't it ridiculous to think of the entire world as somehow alive?

So, as it stands, McFague's model for the God-world relationship seems somewhat strained and artificial. But, as we see in the next chapter, Alfred North Whitehead believes that "the final real things of which the world is made up" are subjects of experience somewhat akin to ourselves from moment to moment.[13] That is, everything that exists is either itself a subject of experience or what Whitehead calls a "society" of such subjects of experience. Not just human beings and other higher-order animals with self-awareness, therefore, but all forms of animal and plant life, even inanimate things, are thus internally composed of mini-subjects of experience (equivalently, spiritual "atoms") with a given pattern of interrelated existence and activity. The individual subjects of experience keep changing, coming into and going out of existence very rapidly, but the societies that they constitute remain the same. Each of us, for example, feels that we are the same person as a moment ago even though subtle changes have taken place within our minds and bodies in just that small time interval. Similarly, within the animals, plants, and even inanimate things of this world, subtle changes are taking place at every moment even as outwardly they all seem to remain much the same.

What emerges out of this Whiteheadian approach to reality is a third model for the God-world relationship that seems to have all the advantages of the model proposed by McFague and very few, if any, of its disadvantages. This third model is based on the notion of a cosmic community in which everything that exists is both itself and partner with everything else to make up a common living space, a community in which to live together. Especially if we think of God not as one person in dialogue with creatures but as three persons who are already in their own divine life even apart from creation a community, the idea of the God-world relationship as a cosmic community makes a lot of sense.[14] In creating us, the three divine persons thus invite us into their living space, their divine communitarian life, insofar as we finite creatures can share in it. Heaven, in other words, is all around us even though in this life we do not fully realize where we are. Limited as we are by the concerns of life in the body here and now under the conditions of space and time, we lose the bigger picture of what is really going on.

In a later chapter of this book, I explain how at the moment of death we will indeed see the bigger picture. But for now I simply clarify how this model is better than the other two for explaining the God-world relationship. Aquinas's model was good for making clear how God is present to every creature as its First Cause or Creator, but he could not do justice to Saint Paul's claim that in God we live and move and have our being. Sallie McFague, using the metaphor of the soul/body relationship, indicated how God is at work in the world in the same way that the soul is in touch with the body. But her metaphor seemed to draw God and the world into too close a relationship with a consequent loss of independence for both God and ourselves. The attractiveness of this third model is that it allows the three divine persons and all of us creatures to be ourselves as separate subjects of experience and yet by our interaction with one another to co-create a common space, a cosmic community to which each and every creature contributes and upon which each and every creature at the same time depends. For the common space or community collapses unless everyone works to sustain it.

This does not mean, of course, that the three divine persons depend upon us creatures for their own existence as in Sallie McFague's model. For they have their own communitarian life even apart from creation. But it does mean that, if the divine persons choose to create a cosmic community, then they need our cooperation in order to sustain that common space between us and themselves. Communities only come into being when subjects of experience dynamically interact and co-create a common space that is gradually shaped and structured by their ongoing interaction. Equivalently they co-create a common field of activity for their ongoing exchange of information and affective response to one another. What you say and do affects me, and what I say and do affects you. Together we bring into being what Martin Buber in his celebrated book *I and Thou* called "the Between," an intangible but very real link between us that lasts as long as we remain in contact with one another on an interpersonal basis.[15] Sometimes we can sense that common space between us while in conversation with others. But, sensed or not, it is always there as the implicit basis for our ongoing relationship.

If then, as Whitehead urges, the world is made up of momentary subjects of experience gathered into "societies," or what I call structured fields of activity, for their ongoing interaction, then the world of creation is made up of an enormous network of hierarchically ordered and overlapping fields of activity for all these created subjects of experience. Just as our own bodies have different levels of activity from the subatomic to the body as a whole, so there are different levels of social organization within the universe (atomic, molecular, organic, supraorganic or environmental, solar systems, galaxies, clusters of galaxies, etc.). Likewise, one and the same subject of experience can participate in more than one society or form of social organization at the same time. Members of a family, for example, create their own special field of activity simply as a family, but they also participate in other communities or other fields of activity by reason of work, political affiliation, or simple friendship. The world for each of us as individuals is a complicated set of overlapping and hierarchically ordered fields of activity that we share with many other individuals, both friends and mere acquaintances.

Furthermore, this entire network of interrelated fields of activity constituting our world is contained within the field of activity proper to the three divine persons. The three divine persons thus set the pattern or provide the structure for what goes on in the world. The New Testament, after all, tells us that we are one with Christ in Christ's relationship to the "Father," all in the power of the "Holy Spirit" (Eph. 1:7–10; Col. 1:15–20). In terms of my own model, that would mean that we human beings and all other created subjects of experience are aligned with the "Son" in the Son's relation to the Father through the mediating power and influence of the Holy Spirit. Like the Son, we too receive from the Father through the activity of the Holy Spirit divine grace at every moment, which both empowers us to be ourselves and lures us in a direction proposed by the Father. Unlike the Son, we all too frequently misuse the divine empowerment and follow our own self-centered inclinations. But the rhythm of life and love among the divine persons still gives a deeper order and purpose to all the myriad decisions made by ourselves and all other created subjects of experience at any given moment of the cosmic process. The world is deeply trinitarian in its overall makeup even though we human beings seldom, if ever, think in those terms.

At the beginning of this chapter, I referred to the importance of different models of the God-world relationship, their significance for the way in which we live our daily lives. What then is the cash value in thinking of the three divine persons, ourselves, and the world of Nature as partners in a cosmic community? In brief, it allows us to see that we do not exist simply for ourselves and our own interests but for the sake of something bigger than ourselves, what Scripture calls the kingdom of God. There is, after all, a basic human instinct first to look out for our own short-range interests and only afterwards to think of the long-term interests of the community (communities) to which we belong. We may label this tendency "original sin" and thus trace it back to the Fall of Adam and Eve in Paradise, or we may attribute it to various conditioning factors in our personal, family, or community history. But in any case it is an all-pervasive tendency in human life. We need a vision of how life can and should be different.

We should find our true self-fulfillment in contributing to a community or cause bigger than ourselves as individuals. This is not to say, of course, that we always have to sacrifice our own interests totally to the interests of the group to which we belong. Quite the contrary, the community exists to serve the needs of all of us, taken collectively. But there will be instances when we will be asked to sacrifice personal interest for what is clearly a higher good representing the future well-being or even continued existence of the group(s) to which we belong. At these moments it is important that we do so willingly rather than under duress because it corresponds more closely to what we recognize as the divine will, the way in which the three divine persons exist among themselves as a divine community and the way in which they seem to have ordered the world of creation in their own image and likeness as a cosmic community destined for ever-deeper communion with themselves.

In Mark's Gospel, James and John, the sons of Zebedee, ask Jesus for privileged places at his right and left hand in the future kingdom. When the other disciples learn of this trick, they are indignant. In reply to them all, Jesus says:

> You know that those who are recognized as rulers over the Gentiles lord it over them, and their great ones make their authority over them felt. But it shall not be so among you. Rather, whoever wishes to be great among you will be your servant; whoever wishes to be first among you will be the slave of all. For the Son of Man did not come to be served but to serve and to give his life as a ransom for many. (Mark 10:42–45)

It requires strong personal conviction regularly to exercise power in terms of empowerment or service of others rather than in terms of control and domination. Such strong conviction, however, normally arises only out of a spirituality or enduring vision of the way things are or at least ought to be. Belief in the Trinity as a communion of divine persons selflessly dedicated to the service of one another and of all their creatures can be the cornerstone of such a communitarian spirituality in which all are united in the service of a common goal and a common set of values.

Our understanding of the God-world relationship, accordingly, is not simply a speculative issue to be thought about occasionally and then set aside for more pragmatic concerns.

Rather, it subtly influences at every moment our attitude to ourselves, other human beings and indeed all of God's creatures even as it also shapes and organizes our felt relationship to God. Thus, if we truly believe that in God we live and move and have our being and that as a result we share with the divine persons in a deeply communitarian way of life together with all of God's creatures, we may be more readily inclined to make the periodic sacrifice of personal self-interest so as to pursue the higher good of sustained life in community. In the end, it is simply a matter of seeing the bigger picture, realizing what life is ultimately all about.

CHAPTER 2

Divine and Human Creativity

NEARLY EVERYONE lays claim to being creative in one or other dimension of her or his life. Some claim to be creative at their professional work, others in hobbies or jobs around the house (e.g., cooking, gardening, amateur photography). But where does such creativity come from, simply from our own natural gifts or as an inspiration from an outside source? Furthermore, is it always productive of good or is it sometimes destructive in its effects? Was Adolf Hitler, for example, creative in the way that he stirred up the German people to embark on a path of self-destruction in the second quarter of the last century? The topic of creativity is intriguing for many reasons, but also confusing because it seems to imply different things to different people in different contexts.

For Whitehead, creativity is a key concept because in his own words it is "the principle of novelty,"[1] the reason that things keep changing in a world always on the move, subtly different at every moment. At the same time, he did not trouble himself about where it came from. It was simply a given in a process-oriented world, a formative principle within things, that which somehow makes them be.[2] As we shall see shortly, there is a logical problem here for the relationship between God as Creator and creativity since Whitehead says elsewhere that even God is a "creature of creativity."[3] But for the moment let us simply note how creativity works within this world according to Whitehead.

Creativity, says Whitehead, is a principle of activity within human beings that enables Tom, Dick, Harry, and the rest of us to be ourselves at every moment through our own innate powers of self-constitution and thereby to contribute to the world around us before we die. This is a commonsense understanding of creativity.

But what is different about Whitehead's approach is that he attributes this power of self-constitution not just to human beings in moments of conscious awareness but in an analogous manner to everyone and everything else as well (animals, plants, even the ultimate components of inanimate things). In Whitehead's view "the final real things of which the world is made up" are what he calls "actual entities" or "actual occasions," that is, momentary self-constituting subjects of experience that combine in different ways to make up all the persons and things, communities and environments, of commonsense experience.[4]

What a crazy idea! Not so, argues Whitehead. The only reality in this world that each of us knows from the inside, so to speak, is ourselves in successive moments of consciousness. And what does consciousness tell us if not that we are at every moment becoming new persons in virtue of all the things that are happening to us and all the decisions (big and small) that we are making as a result. Each moment of consciousness is a new beginning. But it only lasts for a moment, and in the next moment of consciousness we have to do it all over again, become the person of the present moment instead of the person of just a moment ago. Yet all this happens to us only because of the invisible action of creativity in our minds and hearts.

But, you may object, this is contrary to common sense. People do not change that quickly. Nor do animals and plants. For that matter, inanimate things do not seem to change at all; they remain the same for long periods of time. Whitehead's answer is that these actual occasions or momentary subjects of experience have a way of congregating into what he calls "societies" or series of actual occasions with a relatively fixed pattern of existence and activity.[5] Each of us, for example, instinctively feels that we are the same person from moment to moment, but this is because we basically continue to relate to the world around us in the same way from moment to moment. Each of the moments of consciousness is distinct, but it subtly blends into a series of moments with the same pattern of behavior and action so that we have the feeling of being the same person even with minor changes along the way.

Furthermore, most Whiteheadian societies are extended in space as well as in time. Our bodies, for example, as opposed to our consciousness or "soul," take up space as well as endure in time. They are what Whitehead calls "structured societies," that is, societies made up of subsocieties or subfields of activity within the body corresponding to legs, arms, internal organs, and so on. Hence, the actual occasions or momentary subjects of experience making up all these subsocieties experience change much more slowly than the actual occasions making up our self-awareness from moment to moment. But change does take place as we recognize when we at intervals feel hungry, thirsty, tired, or on the contrary, well-filled or refreshed after a good night's sleep. The human body is a very complex network of interrelated parts or members, which in turn are made up of still other parts or members down to the subatomic level of our existence and activity. According to Whitehead, at all these levels there are societies of actual occasions or momentary subjects of experience at work, perpetuating relatively fixed patterns of existence and activity and thereby guaranteeing our ongoing bodily self-identity.

In similar fashion all the living things of this world, plants and animals in enormous abundance, are understood by Whitehead to be structured societies, societies made up of subsocieties or subfields of activity for their constituent actual occasions. Within each subsociety or subfield of activity, these momentary subjects of experience inherit a pattern of existence and activity from their predecessors and pass it on with little or no modification to their successors. Just as in human consciousness, therefore, there is a strong sense of continuity even though each such actual occasion or momentary subject of experience is at least numerically different from both its predecessors and successors. Continuity amid discontinuity is the name of the game everywhere in Nature. As a result, even inanimate things like tables and chairs are structured societies, societies made up of subsocieties of actual occasions or momentary subjects of experience. The tables and chairs, to be sure, are not alive, but their subatomic components are in their own way alive, passing on a given pattern of existence and activity from moment to moment so as to guarantee that the table or chair does not collapse when we put something on it or sit on it.

All this may seem exceedingly strange until we reflect that within Nature things are seldom as they initially appear to be. For example, we look through a microscope and see that our bodies or any other physical organism are a huge colony of interrelated cells and that these cells are themselves composed of dynamically interrelated parts. Or we are told by physicists that tables and chairs are more empty space than solid matter, and yet that in virtue of electromagnetic forces the atoms within the table or chair strongly cohere so as to present to our senses a solid seemingly impenetrable reality. All that Whitehead has done is to add still another level of analysis to what we already know about physical reality from the natural sciences, namely, that subatomic particles are actually made up of actual occasions or momentary subjects of experience rapidly succeeding one another and that everything above the level of subatomic particle, beginning with the atom, is a society of such momentary subjects of experience bound together by a relatively fixed pattern of existence and activity for its constituent parts or members.

These basic insights out of Whitehead's philosophy are repeated and further explained many times over in subsequent chapters of this book. What is important here and now is to focus on creativity as the internal principle at work in all these actual occasions and the societies into which they aggregate. That is, we want to see how creativity functions within human beings and all the other things of this world to keep them moving into an indeterminate future. For Whitehead himself, as already noted, creativity was simply a metaphysical given, something that needs no further explanation since without it there is no way to explain the fact of constant change. Furthermore, even God is a "creature" of creativity, since even God needs creativity to continue to exist.[6]

In that sense, creativity is even more ultimate than God within Whitehead's scheme. But why would he make such an outrageous claim? The answer to that question has to do with the problem of good and evil, in effect, the use of creativity for better or for worse. In *Science and the Modern World*, for example, Whitehead reasons that if creativity is the motive force behind both good and evil decisions by human beings and other creatures, then God must be distinct from creativity so as to control its operations in the world, "to divide the Good from the Evil."[7] Creativity is then what he calls the Ontological Ultimate, that which makes everything including God behave the way it does. God is the Ethical Ultimate, that transcendent personal being who consciously steers creativity in the right direction for all other finite beings. Yet this is still profoundly unsettling to those of us who profess belief in God as Creator of heaven and earth.

There is, however, an alternative explanation, which I have employed for many years now. Creativity is not a reality independent of God but a reality within God. It is the inner nature or basic principle of existence and activity for God; it is what makes God be who and what God is. In the traditional Baltimore Catechism one of the early questions was "Who made me?" and the answer was "God made me." But, as many a child has innocently asked, "Who made God?" The answer to that question cannot be someone or something apart from God since in that case this other reality would be considered God, Creator of heaven and earth. The only suitable answer is that something inside God made God to be who and what God is. God too has a vital source or wellspring of activity within God's very being which makes God to be God. God is indeed the Supreme Being, but even as the Supreme Being God needs an inner act of being, a vital principle of existence and activity, so as to be who and what God is.

Furthermore, if creativity constitutes the inner nature or essence of God, then God is not just one person, but three persons making up a divine community. Whitehead claims that creativity is the principle whereby "[t]he many become one, and are increased by one."[8] As I see it, that means that creativity is operative within God as the principle whereby the three divine persons share life and love with one another for all eternity. The phrase "increased by one" refers then to successive moments of their communal divine life. As a living reality, God too is never exactly the same from moment to moment. The three divine persons continually grow in their knowledge and love both of one another and of all their creatures. This growth, of course, is always positive, never negative. There is no danger that the relations of the three divine persons to one another and to all their creatures will deteriorate and thus that they will someday break up as a community or in any case cease to be worthy of worship by human beings.

But what does all this mean for our understanding of the way in which creativity works in our own lives? It means, in the first place, that we share at every moment in the life of the three divine persons; we share in their own divine creativity. Our share in divine creativity, to be sure, is limited. But, insofar as we are alive and making decisions, however spontaneous and unreflective, at every moment we participate in divine creativity. But, second, this does not mean that we always use divine creativity for a good purpose. We can also use it to do evil. Whereas the three divine persons consistently use creativity "to divide the Good from the Evil," as noted above, we are not so privileged. We feel the burden of self-centered and irresponsible decisions that either we ourselves or those around us have made in the past. So we are clearly prone to use divine creativity for negative as well as positive purposes, to bring about Evil rather than Good.

At the same time the three divine persons remain involved with us in the effort to use creativity for good ends. After all, we share a common world with them as their creatures. Their method of working with us, however, is somewhat different than the way it is customarily portrayed in traditional theology. They do not order us to do what they want but instead seek to persuade us to do what is right through what Whitehead calls divine "initial aims."[9] That is, they first communicate to us the power to make a decision here and now with respect to some future action, but they also offer us a lure toward what is better and away from what is harmful for ourselves and others.[10] In the end, the decision is ours, not theirs. Hence, they are not responsible for our bad decisions even though we could not make the decision for either good or evil without the gift or the grace of divine creativity at every moment. Moreover, they do not give up on us after a few bad decisions on our part but keep helping us to remedy those bad decisions and to set up a new pattern of good decisions. In effect, they suffer with us in our failures and rejoice with us in our successes. But, in either case, they never let us cling to the past. The future in the form of new initial aims for new situations always beckons.

Unlike some traditional understandings of grace, therefore, the divine persons by their gift of grace or divine creativity do not in any way determine or control our decisions; there is no predestination in view of a divine plan for ourselves as individuals or as members of the human race. Instead, the divine persons only seek to persuade us to do what is better for ourselves and others, with considerable latitude given to us on how to specify further the divine lure. In technical language, the work of the divine persons in our regard is primarily in terms of final causality, ordering our individual decisions to some higher goal or value, rather than in terms of efficient causality, making things happen just one way and not some other way. The divine persons still exercise some efficient causality in our regard since, as noted above, they empower us to make our decisions, for better or for worse. But the primary efficient cause in each case is not the three divine persons but we ourselves as we make a decision here and now.[11]

Granted that creativity can move us to do evil as well as good, it remains a special gift from the divine persons since it empowers us to make needed changes in our lives, to move from what already is to what could be in terms of new possibilities. It literally emboldens or encourages us to take a chance on something new and untried even as it likewise reminds us of our limitations in terms of past successes and failures. As Whitehead comments, "Every actual entity, including God, is a creature transcended by the creativity which it qualifies."[12] That is, creativity is always conditioned or "qualified" by our previous decisions even as it empowers us to try something new. In most cases, what is new is as a result only slightly different from what has already happened. But in principle every new moment of experience is an opportunity to start afresh, to experiment with a new pattern of behavior.

This is important not only for the understanding of grace within our lives but also for our traditional image of God. It is rare that we think of God as the source of novelty in our lives; God is rather the transcendent principle of order, carefully limiting or setting bounds to a principle of creativity which seems to spring from our own unbridled imagination and which is thus inherently unstable or sometimes even dangerous. God is the author of the Ten Commandments more than the playful Muse urging us to take a chance on something new. But once we realize that we are engaged in a genuinely intersubjective relationship with the three divine persons, then should we not expect the unexpected?

The beauty of a solid intersubjective relationship between two human beings, after all, is that it is a harmonious blend of order and novelty. If it were entirely orderly and predictable, we would shortly become bored and break off the relationship in search of more exciting companionship. On the other hand, if it were completely dominated by novelty so that we never knew what to expect next from the other person, we would likewise shortly give up the relationship out of sheer fatigue and anxiety. The charm of a solid intersubjective relationship is that it combines order and novelty in ever changing ways so that we simultaneously feel secure in the relationship and challenged by it. Similarly, our relationship with God or the three divine persons should be characterized by an attractive blend of order and novelty, a steady source of comfort in moments of anxiety and yet a spur to venture out into unknown territory, at least at periodic intervals in our lives.

This Whiteheadian principle of creativity also functions as a principle of creative advance within the universe as a whole. It urges all of God's creatures to keep moving, to stay engaged with the surrounding world and to make a contribution to the betterment of that world before passing on. It works within God as well as within the world since creativity likewise serves as the principle of order and novelty for the three divine persons in their relationships to one another within the divine community. Within classical metaphysics, to be sure, the nature of God is simply "to be," that is, to exercise the act of being in its fullness.[13] But what is the act of being if not to combine order and novelty in ever changing ways and thus to live life to the fullest? One of the defects of the classical understanding of the act of being, in my judgment, is that it has been pictured as eternal and unchanging. But is this truly synonymous with what we conventionally mean by life, or is it paradoxically associated with death, the cessation of life? The divine life as the fullness of life must surely be constant and thus in some sense humanly predictable, but it is not for that same reason completely unchanging. It is rather full of novelty for the divine persons, even as our human lives are full of surprises.[14]

In classical theology it is customary to distinguish between moral evil (evil done as a result of bad human decisions) and natural evil (evil that comes about unexpectedly through impersonal forces of nature, such as a hurricane, an earthquake, a tornado, etc.). Because of the enormous suffering frequently thus involved, natural evil prompts us to ask why it happened and whether or not God willed it or at least allowed it to happen. This is not an easy question to answer since we cannot observe and judge how God works in the world of Nature. But, if the divine persons are partly responsible for moral evil because they empower human beings to make bad decisions, perhaps they are also partly responsible for the occurrence of natural evil in the world of Nature.

One could object, of course, that only human beings can make bad decisions; animals, plants, and, above all, the inanimate forces of Nature are part of a vast web of cause-and-effect relations that determine down to the last detail what happens in the world of Nature. Yet this inevitably reduces the world of Nature (including the bodies of human beings) to a cosmic machine in which spontaneity or indeterminacy plays no role. Likewise, even in this case, one can still ask whether God as the Designer of the world machine could not have done a better job. Is God even here not ultimately responsible for natural evil, understood as innocent suffering due to causes over which one has no control?

But if, as Whitehead urges, "the final real things of which the world is made up" are actual occasions or momentary self-constituting subjects of experience, then there is a degree of spontaneity within all of nonhuman nature that corresponds in some limited way to human free will. Hence, nonhuman creatures must likewise share in the blame for natural evil. Just as human beings have to be free to use God-given creativity to make their own decisions, whether for good or for evil, so non-human subjects of experience within nature enjoy a degree of spontaneity that is not entirely predictable. Higher-order animals like household pets seem to have a personality even if they are not making self-conscious decisions after the fashion of human beings. Lower-order animal species (e.g., birds and insects) and various forms of plant life also possess a degree of spontaneity without being conscious of it. They exhibit at times an unpredictability for which there is no apparent rational explanation; they are, after all, not machines but living organisms with some limited ability to adjust to a changing environment. Finally, even among the physical constituents of inanimate realities, e.g., atoms and molecules, there is a surprising level of indeterminacy and unpredictability which, to be sure, normally averages out to produce the apparently unchanging tables and chairs, sticks and stones, of commonsense experience. But as the quantum physicists of the last century discovered to their amazement, classical laws of cause and effect do not apply in this submicroscopic world; there are no strictly predetermined outcomes at the subatomic level. Only statistical probabilities are possible to gauge what will happen next.[15]

God then must be partly responsible for natural evil in this world as well as for moral evil because God is the source of the power of creativity which can be used for evil as well as good decisions by nonhuman creatures. But here too God is constantly at work within the nonhuman world through the provision of divine initial aims to the various actual occasions constituting the living organisms and inanimate things of this world so as to minimize the amount of disorder and destruction that might be caused by their spontaneous decisions. Cancer, for example, is a result of the normal division of cells gone

awry within a given organism. Why does this happen? There is
no fully rational explanation for this occurrence. Chance plays
a role in favorable mutations; chance is equally at work in unfa-
vorable mutations leading to the growth of cancer. The initial
effect of divine initial aims in such a case might well be to minimize the growth of the cancer in its early stages so as to give
doctors and nurses a little more time first to detect the cancer
and then to use drugs and other medical techniques to retard
its rapid growth or even to eliminate it altogether. Medical
miracles do happen, but in most cases it would seem to be a
combination of divine initial aims and human technology that
restores human beings to physical or mental health.

The three divine persons, in other words, have apparently
set in motion a cosmic process in which novelty or spontaneity is present in varying degrees at all levels of existence and
activity. Hence, one should expect things periodically to go
wrong. At the same time, without this provision of novelty and
spontaneity within the creative process, this world would be
far less interesting and full of promise. It would be a world
totally governed by mechanical regularity in which there
would be no room for the new and unexpected. Even if human
beings existed in such a world, they would be just as machine-
like in their existence and activity as every other creature. Free
will would be an illusion since novelty would be sacrificed to
the overriding demand for order and predictability.

Practically speaking, therefore, good and evil must always
coexist. If good and bad decisions are ultimately responsible
for the good and evil to be found in this world, then one must
learn to deal with the latter even as one rejoices in the existence
of the former. The same creaturely decision-making power is
responsible for both. Yet, if the three divine persons value their
own creativity enough to share it in varying degrees with all

their creatures, but above all with us as their rational creatures, then it behooves us to treasure it as our most precious possession even as we in virtue of sometimes painful experience come to the recognition of its destructive as well as creative potential. Creativity is what makes us (and indeed all of creation) godlike. But, improperly used, it is likewise the root cause of the destructive and even demonic features of this world.

CHAPTER 3

The Shape of Things to Come

OVER THE CENTURIES there have been many explanations given for the doctrine of the Incarnation—that one of the divine persons became human and appeared on earth as Jesus of Nazareth. Most of them have been somehow linked with the celebrated passage in John's Gospel that "God so loved the world that he gave his only Son, so that everyone who believes in him might not perish but might have eternal life. For God did not send his Son into the world to condemn the world, but that the world might be saved through him" (John 3:16-17). God became human, in other words, to save human beings from their sins and to bring them to share eternal life with all three divine persons. Yet, even with this common starting-point, there have been different theologies of the redemption over the years. Initial efforts by Saint Augustine, Anselm of Canterbury, and others in the early church focused on an objective explanation of the Redemption. That is, through the passion, death, and resurrection of Jesus an objective change was made in the relationship between God the Father and the Father's rational creatures. Whereas previously human beings experienced only the wrath of God because of their sinful patterns of behavior, now through reliance on the passion and death of Jesus and the grace which he thereby won for humanity, human beings are in a position to work out their salvation with great confidence in God's persevering love for them. Beginning with Peter Abelard in the twelfth century, however, a new theory of the redemption gained credence, namely, that the redemption wrought by Jesus is primarily a subjective reality. The redemption works to the extent that human beings are moved by the example of Jesus to trust in God and to deal compassionately with their brothers and sisters in distress.

Both of these approaches are worthwhile but likewise both appear to be one-sided, in need of further explanation in terms of the other theory. Proponents of the objective theory, for example, fail to account for a necessary subjective change of heart on the part of human beings if they are to appropriate for themselves the objective redemption won for them by Jesus through his passion, death, and resurrection. Proponents of the subjective theory, on the contrary, seem to restrict the objective character of the redemption to the good example offered by Jesus to his followers, thus ignoring the impact of his life, death, and resurrection on the course of human history and indeed on the world of creation as a whole. What is needed is a theory with both an objective and a subjective dimension to the theology of redemption, one that stresses the necessity of a personal conversion to Jesus and his way of life but which also recognizes the way in which human beings routinely influence one another's behavior. In this way the tangible effects of either sinful or grace-filled behavior are passed from one individual to another so as to control over time the thinking and behavior of large groups of people.

Shortly we will see how Jesus met this challenge in his personal life—that is, how he resisted the negative effects of evil and sin among the people around him and thereby gave new focus and direction to the divine plan for the redemption of the human race. But first we review briefly how sin and evil can exist within a world where God is always at work in our lives. As already mentioned in preceding chapters, "the final real things of which the world is made up" are actual occasions, subjects of experience which only last for an instant but in that instant come to a decision (sometimes conscious, most often unconscious) about themselves and their place in the world around them. Every actual occasion anywhere in this world is thus somehow responsible for its own behavior, albeit with help from God in the form of a divine initial aim. It feels the world around it in all its concrete multiplicity and then tries to organize for itself all these feelings in terms of what White-head calls its "subjective aim." Yet its subjective aim may or may not be in conformity with God's purpose for it at this particular moment. God, in other words, proposes to each actual occasion an initial aim or lure toward some purpose or goal on a feeling level. The actual occasion, however, remains free to accept that lure from God or to seek satisfaction through some purpose or goal of its own decision, whether conscious or not.

This is as true of the actual occasions making up a subatomic particle as it is of the actual occasions that constitute consciousness for us human beings. In the case of the subatomic particle, the amount of spontaneity or freedom it enjoys is very limited, since it tends simply to repeat whatever pattern of activity it finds at work in its environment. Within our human consciousness, on the contrary, each actual occasion grasps several different possibilities for self-realization, each of which has its own lure for satisfaction. Hence, an actual occasion within the consciousness of a human being enjoys many more options, so to speak, beyond the one offered by God through the divine initial aim. Whenever such an actual occasion does not conform its subjective aim to the divine initial aim, then it "errs" (on the human level, "sins") and brings about some objective disorder in the world process.

Most of the erring thus done by actual occasions in this world are done by human beings in successive moments of consciousness when they insist on doing things their own way. Yet it is important to realize that evil as an objective disorder within the world process can come into being through the action of creatures other than human beings. Admittedly, within a world governed by evolution and the principle of natural selection, it is difficult to determine whether something that happens in Nature is truly evil or simply the working out of a natural process. Death, for example, especially if it comes at the end of a normal life span, is not an evil, even though it causes pain and anxiety to the individual in question beforehand, and deep sorrow to survivors afterwards. Similarly, as Norman Pittenger suggests, many natural catastrophes (e.g., earthquakes, hurricanes, tornados, even forest fires caused by lightning strikes) are caused by a "natural adjustment" of the forces of nature.[1] Not to allow these adjustments to take place might well precipitate an even greater natural catastrophe in the long run.

But, even allowing for these merely apparent evils within Nature, there still seem to be instances where especially human beings, but sometimes nonhuman creatures as well, deviate from customary patterns of behavior and thereby bring unexpected and seemingly pointless pain and suffering upon themselves and other creatures within their environment. One possible explanation for such deviant behavior would be what I just suggested: namely, that every creature possesses a certain degree of spontaneity or in any case indeterminacy in its self-constitution,[2] so that it can depart from God's aim for it and as a result bring a certain amount of disorder into the cosmic process. As Holmes Rolston suggests, evolution is a "cruciform" process; it only moves forward through a process of trial and error with pain and suffering as an inevitable consequence of making mistakes along the way.[3] But there are also instances where the pain and suffering seem to be totally pointless, without any redeeming after-effects. Here I would argue that, when and if such mindless evil happens, it is due to the misguided decision of the creature rather than as a result of some hidden divine plan.

Given these presuppositions about the occurrence of sin and evil in this world, how are we to understand traditional Christian belief that Jesus by his life, death, and resurrection redeemed the human race and revealed God's plan for a "new heaven and a new earth" (Rev. 21:1)? First of all, let us assume that at every moment of his life Jesus conformed his subjective aim to the initial aim of God for him. By "God" I mean here primarily "God the Father," but secondarily also "God the Son," since Jesus in his human nature was one with the Son in the latter's ongoing response to the Father within the divine communitarian life. As Karl Rahner suggests in *Foundations of Christian Faith*, Jesus' humanity was "the most autonomous and most free" not in spite of, but because it was assumed by the Son, because it had been created as God's self-expression par excellence within the created order.[4] Precisely because Jesus allowed God's initial aim to determine his own subjective aim at every moment of consciousness, he experienced a unique freedom as a human being. He was free, in other words, from all the imbalances in human life that inevitably result from making ill-advised decisions and then rationalizing them afterwards. Jesus was free with the freedom which God the Father intends for all human beings provided that they attend more carefully to the Father's initial aims for them. Jesus, then, presumably grew in self-confidence as he, prompted by the "Holy Spirit," consistently followed the path laid out for him by God the Father and saw the positive influence that he had on other people.

As Peter Hodgson suggests in *New Birth of Freedom*, Jesus was thereby implicitly setting up a new lifestyle, a new model for human behavior.[5] Whereas in the pagan world people thought of freedom primarily in terms of autonomy and self-sufficiency, Jesus evidently conceived freedom for himself in terms of dependence on God as his Heavenly Father and of interdependence with other human beings as his brothers and sisters. He did not see his own freedom as threatened either by the Father's will for him or by the needs of people around him. He gave freely of himself to others because he trusted that the Father would provide for each and all. His exhortation to others was to seek first of all the kingdom of God and its righteousness in the confident expectation that all the practical issues (what to eat, how to be clothed, etc.) would eventually be taken care of (Matt. 6:25–34). Given the fact that he lived the way he preached, namely, as an itinerant preacher dependent upon the alms of other people, the impact of Jesus' message must have been quite powerful. Some, undoubtedly, reacted to it angrily, considering him to be a consummate fool. But others saw in the person of Jesus hope for a new and better way of life for themselves.

Especially in his healing ministry, Jesus touched the minds and hearts of those around him. He cured their physical diseases, but above all he offered them forgiveness of their sins. Thereby he assured them that he cared for them as the unique individuals that they really were. He restored to them the humanity that they had somehow lost in the sordid scramble for the good things of this world. All that he asked in return was that they be as humane to one another as he had been to them, that they extend to one another the same practical forgiveness of sins as he had offered to them. Jesus, to be sure, did have harsh words for certain groups of people in the society of his day. Yet these were not self-confessed sinners but rather hypocrites, individuals who refused to admit that they like everyone else stood in constant need of God's forgiving love. Effectively, they were denying their own humanity. Hence, Jesus felt constrained to warn them of their hardness of heart, which in turn infuriated these individuals and prepared the way for the angry confrontation between Jesus and themselves that would result in Jesus' condemnation and execution as a common criminal. Yet if Jesus ran away or otherwise avoided the painful death which he sensed thus lay in store for him, he would not have been faithful to the Father's purpose for him at that moment of his life, namely, to persevere in loving concern for his fellow human beings even as they put him to death.

Similarly, Jesus had to take a critical stance toward the various social institutions and customs of his day that reflected a basic imbalance in the human psyche. His personal freedom from these social pressures gave him unexpected insight into these social ills but also laid upon him a heavy responsibility to denounce them as opportunity arose. For example, as Lisa Sergio points out, Jesus saw with an aching heart the degraded position of women in the society of his day and tried to adjust the balance.[6] When his enemies brought to him a woman caught in the act of adultery to see whether he would approve her being stoned to death, Jesus at first said nothing but then finally responded, "If there is one of you who has not sinned, let him be the first to throw a stone at her" (John 8:7). Thereby he reminded them that they too were sinners and, even more pointedly, that the woman had not committed adultery alone. Where then was the man, and why was he not also brought before Jesus for condemnation?[27] Jesus, of course, did not condone the woman's sin, anymore than he condoned the sins of human beings anywhere. But, when they were alone, he made clear to her that her sin was indeed forgiven and that it lay within her power to reform her life. Thereby he restored her humanity, her sense of self-worth precisely as a woman.

Still another instance of Jesus' persistent good sense and sound judgment is evident in his battle with certain Scribes and Pharisees over the issue of the Sabbath observance. When they brought to him a man with a withered hand on the Sabbath day and asked whether it was legitimate to cure him and others like him on the official day of rest, he first reminded them that they would have no scruple in rescuing a drowning animal from a well on the Sabbath and then added, "Now a man is far more important than a sheep, so it follows that it is permitted to do good on the sabbath" (Matt. 12:12). On another occasion he remarked even more incisively, "The sabbath was made for man, not man for the sabbath" (Mark 2:27). At stake here, of course, was a key imbalance in the lives of those who prided themselves upon the exact external observance of the Jewish Law. Jesus also reverenced the Law as divinely revealed. Yet at the same time he recognized that there would inevitably be circumstances when observance of the letter of the Law would be contrary to its spirit, in which case one should be free not to observe the Law.

In the political arena, Jesus likewise showed a rare balance, a singular freedom from involvement in causes which, though worthwhile in themselves, carried with them the threat of strictly partisan action and especially for himself possible misuse of his messianic power. For example, he saw the futility of the dreams of the Zealots and other Jewish revolutionaries for political and economic independence, given the status of subject nations within the Roman Empire of his day. But, quite independently of that, he knew intuitively that his own mission as Messiah would be frustrated if he and his followers resorted to force to bring about the eschatological kingdom of God. Since the good news of salvation was to be preached to all, rich as well as poor, rulers as well as subjects, he had to show himself as well-disposed toward all segments of Jewish society. Accordingly, he preached to both rich and poor the need for independence from the craving for more and more money (Mark 10:17–31). For both rulers and ruled, he set forth the ideal of service to others as the only way to sublimate the instinctive human craving for domination and control (Mark 10:35–45; see also Matt. 20:20–28; Luke 22:24–27). Through such nonviolent means he hoped to set in motion a social revolution of enormous proportions, but he cherished no illusions that this revolution would be accomplished within his own lifetime. In every conflict situation he listened for that inner voice, the divine initial aim from the Father, which told him how to be all things to all women and men of goodwill.

Listening to the voice of conscience clearly became more important for Jesus as his public ministry progressed. At first, obedience to that divine prompting gave him great joy as he witnessed the impact that he was having upon people through his message and miracles, but as time went on he felt a growing hostility from still other groups of people. Precisely because he challenged the status quo on so many points by both his words and example, he represented a real threat to those individuals whose vested interests, for whatever reason, lay in carefully protecting that same status quo. Here Jesus faced a real conscience crisis. If he chose to compromise with the powers-that-be, they would surely not inhibit his work of preaching and healing among the masses. Yet on key issues he would have to be ambivalent and thus blunt the full force of his message to others. If he chose the route of confrontation with evil wherever he met it, he would probably meet a violent end at the hands of those same powers-that-be. He would sooner or later suffer the fate of so many prophetic figures in Israelite history and thus see his mission in life, the preaching of the kingdom, come to a tragic end.

Characteristically, in this moment of crisis Jesus chose to listen to his inner voice. Since the Father seemed to be urging confrontation rather than compromise with the powers-that-be, Jesus focused his preaching more and more on various forms of social evil in the society of his day. At the same time, he urged upon his followers a momentous choice: "If anyone wants to be a follower of mine, let him renounce himself and take up his cross and follow me. For anyone who wants to save his life will lose it, but anyone who loses his life for my sake, and for the sake of the Gospel, will save it" (Mark 8:34–35; Matt. 16:24–28; Luke 9:23–26). Here then was the paschal mystery or the Father's plan of salvation at work in Jesus' life and preaching long before the dramatic events in Jerusalem that actually produced his death. Jesus did not long to die; on the contrary, he wished to live, to enjoy life in its fullness with his friends. But he recognized that obedience to his Father's will as revealed in the inner voice of conscience was the only sure way to true self-fulfillment. Hence, he felt obliged to follow it, even though he recognized with a heavy heart that his life in all likelihood would be considerably shorter as a result. Furthermore, he urged upon his followers the same weighty choice: to choose life, but life in accord with the Father's plan for the salvation of the world, not life as one would ideally choose to live it in some utopian existence.

The touchstone for the paschal mystery, then, both as it operated in the human consciousness of Jesus prior to his death and resurrection, and as it continues to operate in our own lives to this day, is a life of obedience and self-surrender to the Father.[8] With divine wisdom the Father foresees what will be the cost in terms of pain and anxiety for those who seek to live in response to his will for them from moment to moment. But this seems to be only way that the three divine persons can incorporate creatures into their own communitarian life and thereby bring about the redemption of the human race and the transformation of the material universe promised in sacred Scripture. As Arthur McGill points out, between the Father and the Son within the divine communitarian life "there exists a relationship of total and mutual self-giving."[9] The Father gives everything to the Son, but the Son in turn gives his entire being back to the Father, all in the self-giving power of the Holy Spirit. Hence, it is clear that Jesus could not have been the Son of God become incarnate in this world without full surrender of himself to the Father and the Father's will. Likewise, the divine persons must ask of us what they asked of Jesus: namely, to share in the redemption of a fallen world through participation in the exercise of divine power, the power of self-giving love for others.

Yet is self-giving love really that effective in solving the problems of this world? Naturally, self-giving love helps to eliminate various forms of gratuitous violence among human beings. The desire to serve rather than be served (Mark 10:45; Matt. 20:28) tends to sublimate deeply rooted instincts among us for control and domination of others, by force if necessary. But isn't it true that, at least in most such cases, "nice guys

THE SHAPE OF THINGS TO COME · 39

finish last"? Jesus' own earthly life, after all, ended in failure because he refused to use violence even in self-defense. Simply to appeal to Jesus' subsequent resurrection from the dead is likewise not enough to vindicate his life of self-giving love. For, taken by itself, the resurrection seems to be a phony happy ending to an otherwise tragic story. On the contrary, the resurrection only makes sense if it is the ultimate testimony to God's persevering love for us, even when we seem determined to resist that love. It is one last appeal to human beings to give up trying to control their own destinies and like Jesus to surrender in perfect trust to the Father and the Father's will for us even in our darkest hour.

Recall how Jesus had to struggle before bringing his will into conformity with the will of the Father. Death is under any circumstances a fearful experience because it represents a letting go of one's earthly ego, surrendering to an unknown future. Death robs us of control of our lives. Death, however, was especially painful for Jesus since it represented a completely ignominious end to his own life project, preaching the kingdom of God to his fellow Jews. It must have taken enormous trust on his part to accept the fact that death under these circumstances would ultimately be more efficacious for the spread of the kingdom than one in which he would have converted his fellow Jews en masse and employed them as missionaries to spread the good news of God's forgiving love throughout the world. Perhaps that is why both in the garden of Gethsemane the night before and again hanging on the cross on Calvary the next day Jesus agonized through a period of extreme self-doubt before coming to terms with his fate and submitting to his Father's will in this matter as indeed in all the other choices of his life. Yet without this ultimate self-renunciation the resurrection could not have taken place.

Jesus had to follow through with the Father's plan for him.

In similar fashion, the rest of us find ourselves regularly faced with an awkward choice: either to pursue single-mindedly our own goals and values in life with scant attention to the needs and desires of others or to live in a responsive relation to the Father and the Father's initial aims for us as part of the divine plan for the redemption of the human race and the transformation of the world around us. Admittedly, this sometimes seems like spiritual "death," a total loss of one's autonomy, one's independence of judgment and action. Yet paradoxically it results in a higher form of self-fulfillment for those who have the courage to live as Jesus did. On the contrary, those who pursue strictly self-centered interests and desires and thus appear to be living life to the fullest here and now are actually the ones who are spiritually dying since they are gradually losing a sense of purpose and value in life because of their refusal to cooperate with the Father's plan for them.[10] Only if in imitation of Jesus we are prepared to lose our lives for the sake of the kingdom of God will we gain eternal life in union with the divine persons. In that sense, the life, death, and resurrection of Jesus represent for us as his followers "the shape of things to come."

CHAPTER 4

The Collective Power of Good and Evil

THUS FAR we have indicated how the paschal mystery, the self-giving love of God, works within the hearts and minds of ourselves as individuals. Now it is time to consider the operation of the paschal mystery within communities, how it functions to open us up as members of communities in self-giving love to one another. But beforehand we must take an honest look at the way that human communities all too often end up dividing us from one another. In a word, we must first analyze what I call the collective power of evil as it comes to expression in the day-to-day functioning of human communities as they all too often engage in unholy competition with one another for power and influence. Only then will we understand how the paschal mystery is the focus of the collective power of good in this world. Likewise, only then will we see why God had to become human so as to give new energy and direction to the collective power of good in this world.

Let me begin, however, by eliminating a possible misunderstanding. The collective powers of good and evil are not separable into two different communities that are completely opposed to one another. On the contrary, all human communities (even the church, as we shall see below) are a mixture of good and evil; hence, each of them contributes by its mode of operation to the collective power of evil as well as to the collective power of good in this world. Human beings, for example, join together in community because they are animated by a common spirit. They feel a need to pool their time and energy, their resources both material and spiritual, in order to achieve common goals. All this is praiseworthy and good since it corresponds to the deeply rooted desire within us to share life with others, to find self-fulfillment through belonging to a group. If, however, the goals of the group are too narrowly focused with little or no concern for the legitimate needs and desires of other individuals and other groups, then membership in the community tends to reinforce the self-centered and sinful tendencies already present in us as individuals. As Reinhold Niebuhr notes, a group can be "more arrogant, hypocritical, self-centered and more ruthless in the pursuit of its ends than the individual."[1] Especially when the community finds itself in direct competition with other communities for achievement of basically the same goals and values, its members feel justified, out of loyalty to the community, to use whatever means are thought necessary to guarantee its survival and well-being.

Similarly, within communities subgroups are often struggling for power and control. When one subgroup temporarily wins the power struggle it will promote the common good, to be sure, but only insofar as it serves its own best interests. Sensing the partiality that has thus crept into the government of the community, other groups will strive to unseat the individuals currently in power so as to direct the community along new lines more favorable to their interests. On one level, there is nothing wrong with such a power game. It is part of the art of politics, provided that each group plays fair, uses tactics that are legal and open to public scrutiny. But the danger always exists that one group will use illegal or even immoral methods to gain the upper hand, and that the other groups will then feel justified in employing the same or similar methods themselves. Then a healthy rivalry between different interest groups for the leadership of the community becomes instead a really bitter power struggle in which each side seeks to eliminate altogether the power of other groups within the community. Such a situation is evil, not because power is a factor here, but because it is being used to unfair advantage against groups and individuals who are for the moment powerless.[2]

Once again, I am not suggesting that something is intrinsically evil about life in community. We human beings cannot survive, much less prosper, without the encouragement and assistance of other people, beginning with the members of our immediate family. But, like ourselves as individuals, communities have a sinful side as well as a grace-filled side, a proneness to narrow self-interest as well as to openhearted self-giving. This self-preoccupation disguises itself as the perfectly legitimate need of a community (or of a subgroup within a community) to protect itself against attack from others to guarantee its own survival. But it is easy then for an us-versus-them mentality to prevail so that out of fear of being dominated by others community members end up consciously or unconsciously taking unfair advantage of others.

Very much as individuals sin by yielding to self-centered interests and desires rather than by following divine initial aims from the "Father," so communities "sin" in and through the collective actions of their own members in dealing with individuals belonging to other groups. Furthermore, community members tend to lie to themselves as to why they behave as they do. That is, since they are reluctant to admit openly their desire for power and control over others (or, more likely, their deep-rooted fear of powerlessness, being controlled by others), they preach to one another, and to anyone else who will listen, a carefully contrived justification of what to an outsider can only be seen as arrogant, hypocritical, self-centered behavior. Since they receive little or no criticism from others within the community, they easily convince themselves that they are speaking the truth and react very negatively to anyone who questions the objectivity and truthfulness of their remarks.

In more traditional theological language, what I am describing here could be labeled "original sin." But the classical notion of original sin seems to place the blame for the existence of evil in this world on individuals in isolation rather than on individuals as members of specific communities. The term "collective power of evil," however, focuses on the sinfulness that pertains to the individual insofar as he or she belongs to a given community and uncritically accepts whatever might be the negative spirit or hostility of the community toward nonmembers or rival groups. Here is where racial prejudice and covert discrimination against women and various minority groups have their origin. The individual, to be sure, contributes to the formation and preservation of such a negative spirit within the group by his or her personal behavior. But prior to any personal decision, the individual is already strongly influenced by the prevailing mind-set of the group. In this sense, the traditional notion of original sin as a preconscious bias toward sinful or self-centered behavior is better conveyed by the term "collective power of evil" when the focus is on the workings of communities rather than on the actions of individuals.

Arthur McGill makes the case that demonic evil is just as strongly present in modern life as it was in the life of Jesus and his contemporaries.[3] That is, Jesus was clearly engaged with the powers of darkness through his healing miracles and exorcisms. But, says McGill, contemporary human beings likewise experience the demonic in terms of mindless violence or at least the ever-present threat of mindless violence. "People today see in such violence the operation of forces that are peculiarly and essentially destructive, and that no properly human kind of power is able to withstand."[4] McGill published his book in 1968 during the Vietnam War and at the time of race riots in the United States. But his message is even more pertinent since September 11, 2001, when the World Trade Towers in New York City were demolished by terrorists and the possibility of further terrorist acts within their own country became a vivid reality for all Americans.

McGill's proposed solution to the threat of mindless violence in our time is to follow the example of Jesus in the Gospel narratives, to refuse to meet violence with even more violence. But he also makes clear how difficult that is in our contemporary Western culture where there is so much violence reported in the news media and where the portrayal of violence has become a common theme in the entertainment industry (television, motion pictures, and in recent years video games). Unhappily, since McGill wrote his book, events on the international scene have made matters even worse. Efforts on the part of governments to halt or control mindless violence by terrorists through further acts of violence undertaken in the name of national security seem in the end only to contribute to an all-pervasive culture of violence together with a deep sense of anxiety that ordinary people feel in the face of what they cannot personally prevent or control.

A collective power of good that will effectively counteract the wide-ranging influence of the collective power of evil in contemporary society, then, will only be sustained through the efforts of people who are in principle nonviolent toward one another. I say "in principle" deliberately because in practice there inevitably arise situations in which people must use limited forms of violence in order to halt or at least control even greater violence directed against themselves and others under their care and protection. But, even when they have to resort to such limited violence, these people recognize that violence in any form represents a breakdown in normal human relations and that, if continued for any but the most serious reasons, even such limited violence will only lead to greater violence—in effect, initiating an unending cycle of violence. Hence, even if compelled by circumstances to resort to limited violence, these individuals are still resisting the influence of the collective power of evil in their lives. They do not accept the notion of casual violence, that violence in some form or other is part of the normal pattern of human life. Contrary to what one might assume from watching prime-time television and many Hollywood films, violence is not the preferred way to assert oneself in dealing with other people.

Because it is so hard to be consistently reasonable and patient with other people, because it is so easy to feel isolated in one's efforts to adhere to a policy of nonviolence in dealing with others, it seems reasonable to suppose that the deeper reason for the Incarnation, the appearance in human history of the Divine Word as redeemer of the human race, was (and still is) to give new focus and added strength to the collective power of good in the world. Presumably the thought of an all-encompassing community of people who on principle deal with one another nonviolently has been present, at least as a visionary ideal, in the minds and hearts of good people from the very beginning of human history. But human life in community gradually became more complicated as human beings found themselves involved in larger and more intricate social arrangements. As this happened, the temptation grew to subordinate the ideal order of things to more pragmatic interests and desires—in effect, out of a desire for power and control or simply in the interests of individual and group survival—and to yield to the collective power of evil in the manner described above. At a critical juncture in the history of the human race, then, the Divine Word had to become incarnate so as to resist in his own person and through the power of his preaching and example the collective power of evil in human minds and hearts, which was slowly but surely undermining their natural desire for life in community with one another.

As Pierre Teilhard de Chardin noted some years ago, the last six thousand years of human history have seen an enormous growth in human communication and socialization, that is, the organization of human beings into identifiable economic and political units (villages, towns, cities, nations, etc.).[5] Given the increased possibilities for both good and evil which were thus made available to human beings, it seems logical to conclude that the Divine Word chose to become incarnate at a critical point in this same historical process. If the ideal of a unified human race, people living in peace and harmony with one another, was ever to be a reality, then at some point in human history a conscious focus in that direction had to be established. A way had to be found to mobilize the forces for good in this world, which were slowly giving way to the collective power of evil as manifest in the various distorted forms of human community existent in the world at the time of Jesus.

Even if what we say is true, this task was one that Jesus clearly could not have accomplished by himself. He had to enlist the aid of other people to preach the good news of salvation, that is, that God is a loving Father and that one can, accordingly, turn over the direction of one's life to such a

Father in the confident expectation that others will do the same and that thereby the kingdom of God on earth will truly be established. Even as he gathered disciples about him and sent them out in a preliminary way to preach this message to their fellow Jews, however, Jesus must have been uneasily aware that, if things went wrong, his mission in life would ironically likewise contribute to the growth and development of the collective power of evil in the world. That is, if his fellow Jews did not as a group accept the message that he and his disciples were preaching—if instead the Jewish religious authorities were somehow involved in his death at the hands of the Romans and later questioned the right of his followers to still belong to the synagogue—then those same followers of Jesus would have no choice but to organize themselves into a new sect separate from their fellow Jews. Thus the community of disciples that Jesus presumably had in mind to be the new focus of the collective power of good in the world would subtly be affected in its ongoing self-definition and mode of operation by the collective power of evil, namely the felt need to control and dominate rather than be controlled and be dominated.

There is, of course, no way at this point in history to be sure what Jesus originally had in mind when he began his public life. Yet it is significant that Jesus, as the Gospels present him, did not preach the church but rather the kingdom. The few passages where indirect reference is made to the future church (e.g., Matt. 16:13–20; 18:15–18) are controversial since it is not clear how much the early Christian community may have altered the story of the original event or the teaching of Jesus to suit its own sectarian purposes.[6] In any event, the Jesus of the Gospels gives no indication of wanting to abrogate Judaism. Rather his intent seems to have been to purify it of its exaggerated legalism, presumably so as to make it an apt instrument for a broader purpose, namely the conversion of the Gentile world to the worship of the one true God. The main thrust of Jesus' preaching of the kingdom, after all, was the Fatherhood of God and the new status of men and women everywhere as God's most dear children. For this purpose, Judaism with its long history of dealings with Yahweh as a loving Father was ideally suited, provided that the Jewish people could sufficiently expand their vision of what it meant to be God's chosen people.

In any event, reviewing the history of Christianity from its earliest beginnings, one wonders how much the institutional church has been unconsciously affected by the collective power of evil. As we read in the Acts of the Apostles, Saint Paul and other missionaries to the Gentile world had to fight for the unique identity of Christianity vis-à-vis Judaism, the older and more established religion to which it was so heavily indebted. Likewise, in spreading out across the Roman Empire, messengers of the gospel were constantly confronting the votaries of the various pagan religions that were active at the time. Here too there was a contest for the minds and hearts of human beings with the result more often than not that the differences between Christianity and these other religions rather than their underlying similarities were highlighted. Accordingly, a spirit of sectarianism inevitably developed among Christians which in its own way was at cross-purposes with the message originally preached by Jesus during his earthly life: the Fatherhood of God, the need for all men and women to live together in peace and harmony as the Father's most dear children, the universal character of the kingdom, and so on.

Finally, if we look at the divisions that have arisen within Christianity itself over the centuries—first, the division between Rome and the Eastern Orthodox churches, then the still greater division between Rome and the Protestant denominations—it becomes painfully clear that institutional Christianity cannot simply be identified with the collective power of good in the world, that visionary group of women and men who are dedicated to the overriding purpose of bringing about the kingdom of God on earth. Insofar as the various Christian denominations have been engrossed in the struggle to survive as precisely this or that institution (in opposition to other religious groups), then they are subtly affected by the collective power of evil as described above, just like all other human communities and secular organizations around the world.[7] Once again, competition among rival groups for the same goals and values is not evil in itself, but it rapidly becomes evil when survival at all costs is the norm.

I conclude now with some personal reflections on the way in which the collective power of good and the collective power of evil work in our own lives. It is important to realize that we cannot escape being heavily influenced by these two supra-individual realities. In different ways each of them affects everything we say and do, but for the same reason we should not be judgmental about the thinking and behavior of those around us. They too, like us, find it difficult to resist the apparent pragmatism of the collective power of evil and to embrace without reserve the idealism represented by the collective power of good. Likewise, as I indicated above, the church is affected by the collective power of evil even as it quite properly sees itself as the focal point for the collective power of good in the world. Religious communities, much like their individual members, tend to spend altogether too much time worrying about corporate survival and not nearly enough time seeking the Father's will for the group and here and now trying to serve the neighbor in need.

In particular, those in charge of the church and other religiously oriented communities seem much too frequently to be inwardly rather than outwardly focused. As a result, they are psychologically not in a position to take advantage of divine creativity communicated to them through initial aims from the Father. As we noted in an earlier chapter, divine creativity is in the first place a principle of novelty within the world process. It urges us judiciously but still insistently to try something new, not simply to adhere to the status quo, since in barely noticed ways the world around us is always changing and fresh insights are required to adjust to what is no longer the same as before. The church is always in need of reform, but this reform is best carried on by communities of people who habitually listen for the promptings of the divine Spirit. In particular, church leaders should realize that the Spirit speaks not only to themselves as shepherds of the flock but to laypeople as well. The view "from below" is not necessarily better than the view "from above," but it certainly deserves an honest hearing in deciding on church policy. In either case, both clergy and laity should be aware how the collective power of evil subtly asserts itself in the implicit desire to control and dominate rather than to be controlled and dominated.

In the end, then, awareness of the ongoing coexistence of the collective power of good and of evil in this world should make us humble in assessing our own contribution to the coming of God's kingdom. In Luke 16:13, to be sure, Jesus is recorded as saying "No servant can serve two masters. He will either hate one and love the other, or be devoted to one and despise the other." But, as I see it, most of us do serve two masters on a regular basis, both the collective power of good and the collective power of evil. The real question is which one do we love even when we are periodically unfaithful in its service, and which one do we despise even as we yield to the lure of its arguments in a given instance. Provided that we continue to love the person of Jesus and what he stands for in terms of the collective power of good, we are still on the way to salvation for ourselves and those around us. Only when we despise the call of Jesus as impractical and unrealistic are we in danger of permanently losing the deeper meaning and value of our lives on earth and of our enduring relationship to God.

CHAPTER 5

The Church and the Kingdom of God

IN CHAPTER 13 of Matthew's Gospel, Jesus instructs his disciples about the kingdom of God in a long series of parables. But why did he talk in parables, which are always somewhat ambiguous as to their meaning and application to ordinary life? Why didn't Jesus express more directly what he meant by the kingdom? One good reason is that the term "kingdom" was politically charged for Jesus' contemporaries. They resented the Roman occupation of their land together with the taxes that they were obliged to pay as a result of the occupation. Thus anyone who preached about a kingdom in days to come apart from Roman rule would be received enthusiastically by some but with great suspicion by the Roman authorities and their collaborators at the time. Hence, Jesus had to be careful to keep his remarks about the kingdom somewhat vague so that he would not be arrested for conspiracy to overthrow the Roman rule.

But, even more importantly as I see it, Jesus was trying to describe a reality that could not be grasped in ordinary commonsense terms. The only way that he could present it was through stories that were on first hearing quite incredible, a real shock to his listeners. Then, jarred out of their customary ways of thinking, they might make an imaginative leap and intuitively grasp what Jesus had in mind, get a feeling for something that in many cases seemed too good to be true. The first such parable, for example, was the story of the Sower of the Seed. Given their own experience of how one goes about sowing seeds in a field, Jesus' listeners could readily understand how some of the seed was wasted because it fell on poor ground. But they would have been stunned to hear that the seed that fell on good ground "produced fruit, a hundred or sixty or thirty fold" (Matt. 13:18). Such an abundant harvest simply did not happen in the normal course of events.

In similar fashion, the parable of the Weeds among the Wheat defied conventional wisdom. One does not let weeds and wheat grow together until harvest time. The weeds deprive the wheat of much of the nutrients from the soil that the wheat needs to yield a good harvest. Likewise, one does not sell all that one has in this world to purchase a single field or a single pearl. Too much is at stake if one makes a mistake in assessing the value of the treasure hidden in the field or the commercial value of the single pearl on the open market. What, then, can the kingdom of God be that it can be attained only at such a high risk? Finally, still other parables like the Growth of a Mustard Seed or the Expansion of Yeast in Dough point to the kingdom as something that is not yet here in its fullness but still will infallibly come if people only trust in its eventual coming. Without antecedent faith in Jesus and his message, one would be inclined to dismiss these parables as not worthy of serious attention.

In the next few pages I present my own parable, or more precisely my own model for what is meant by the term "kingdom of God." Initially, it may seem quite unlikely but I urge the reader to think it through and see whether it produces an imaginative leap such as described above. In brief, I picture the kingdom of God as the space or field of activity co-created by the three divine persons and all their creatures since the beginning of time. It is not empty space but a field of activity continuously structured by the decisions of all the subjects of experience or actual occasions (both divine and creaturely) in their dynamic relations with one another. There are, in other words, enduring patterns in this field, beginning with the pattern of the relations between the divine persons in their own life apart from creation but then supplemented by the patterns of their interaction with all their creatures, but especially with men and women as their rational creatures. The kingdom of God is a network of relationships that have stood the test of time and that in retrospect have given meaning and value not simply to human history but to the whole course of cosmic evolution from the moment of the Big Bang onward.

Why is it so important to think of the kingdom of God as a common space or structured field of activity between ourselves and the divine persons? The function of space in human life is both to separate and to unite, to give us room to be ourselves and yet to give us a place to be together for mutual interaction. We want closeness with other people but we likewise want others to respect our privacy, the space we need to express ourselves in the way that we prefer. In similar fashion, if the three divine persons invite us into their own communitarian life, they have to give us space to be ourselves so as to respond freely to their divine initiatives in our regard. The three divine persons themselves, after all, give each other plenty of space even as they are most intimately involved with one another as members of the divine community. Their relationships to one another both set them off from each other as "Father," "Son," and "Holy Spirit," and yet join them together in a bond that cannot be broken. They share a common field of activity perfectly and thus are one God, not three gods in close association. Yet each of them exists and is active in that common field of activity in a totally unique way.

In similar fashion, the three divine persons give each of us and the communities to which we belong plenty of space to be ourselves and to relate freely both to the divine persons and to one another. Besides, thinking of the kingdom of God as the space which we occupy both with the divine persons and with one another, we can see much more clearly the role of the church within the kingdom of God. It is not simply identical with the kingdom but rather is one of the key subfields of activity within the kingdom. In fact, given the wide variety of people who call themselves Christian, the church is not a single field within the kingdom but a vast network of fields that are closely interconnected by reason of common rituals and beliefs. There are likewise subfields of activity within the kingdom corresponding to the other world religions and their members. Finally, there are subfields of activity within the kingdom that have no obvious religious orientation but still form part of the pattern and structure of the world around us: physical fields corresponding to the living and nonliving things of this world, intentional fields of activity corresponding to the political and economic structures of our human life-world, and so on. Most of these fields of activity overlap and interpenetrate so that the same actual occasions or subjects of experience find themselves engaged in more than one field of activity at the same time. Taken collectively, all these fields of activity for subjects of experience (divine and created) co-constitute the common space or overall structured field of activity that Christians and other believers in God call the kingdom of God on earth.

In the last chapter we spent time analyzing the workings of

the collective power of good and the collective power of evil in this world. How do these two suprahuman forces fit into this model for understanding the kingdom of God? The collective power of good is the way in which all creatures, but above all we human beings, by our ongoing decisions in response to divine initial aims contribute to the gradual building up of the structure of the kingdom of God. We thereby assist the divine persons in their efforts to incorporate us more fully into their own communitarian life. The collective power of evil, on the contrary, is the way in which all creatures, but especially human beings, thwart the efforts of the divine persons here and now to bring us into the fullness of the divine life. For the moment at least, by our decisions we destabilize the reality of the kingdom of God on earth. Fortunately, the three divine persons are very patient in dealing with their creatures and keep looking for ways to reorient us toward the collective power of good and the kingdom of God without depriving us of our spontaneity or freedom to be what we want to be at every moment. Yet, without the encouragement and assistance of other like-minded individuals, we tend to follow the path of least resistance and pursue short-term goals and values that lead us away from the kingdom of God rather than toward it.

Many years ago Bernard Lee wrote a book entitled *The Becoming of the Church* in which he used the philosophy of Whitehead to make clear how a group of people either become more of what they should be as a church or community of people dedicated to the person and message of Jesus or, on the contrary, how they negatively influence one another so as to fall further away from full adherence to Jesus and his message. Whitehead himself said that while "the final real things of which the world is made up" are actual occasions or momentary subjects of experience, they regularly join together to form "societies" or groups of such actual occasions with a common pattern of self-organization for the constituent actual occasions. As Lee realized, on the level of human communities, the members of a given community thus have a very strong influence on one another's attitudes and behavior.

Once an individual has become a member of a human community, the overall lifestyle of the group maintains its hold on him in virtue of his paying attention to the way others in the group are thinking and behaving.[1] At the same time, the individual, once he or she has assimilated and interiorized this pattern of thinking and behavior, becomes a source of strength and community solidarity to other members, both new and old. In other words, the members of a community see in one another the basic form of life for the group—that is, the ideals, purposes, and values which they hold in common and which they consciously or unconsciously seek to implement in all their dealings with one another. Without such an operative life pattern, individuals no longer feel any strong common bond with one another, and the community will sooner or later cease to exist.

Yet, as already noted in an earlier chapter, the life pattern of most human communities, including the various Christian denominations, is heavily conditioned by the need for survival. Much of the idealism that is resident in the overall purposes and values of the group is inevitably subordinated to the even more basic need to survive in competition with other groups of roughly the same character, with the same purpose and values. Hence, while great good is still unquestionably done by each of these communities, nevertheless much more good could be done if less time and energy were spent in ultimately futile forms of self-preservation. Christian communities, in particular, should take more seriously Lee's advice to make the

"Jesus-event" the pattern or in Whiteheadian terms the "common element of form" for the interrelation of their members with one another.[2]

The "Jesus-event" is Lee's term for the entire life of Jesus, insofar as it revealed or gave expression to a way of thinking and acting from which Jesus never deviated up to the moment of his death. As we have already seen, Jesus participated in the self-giving love proper to the communitarian life of the three divine persons by conforming his subjective aim to the Father's initial aim or purpose for him at every moment of his life. Likewise, he saw his mission in life to be preaching the kingdom and its nearness to all human beings, if only they would repent of their self-centered ways and begin to listen more carefully to the divine initial aim, the voice of God, in their minds and hearts.[3] Those who heed the example of Jesus and mold their lives after the pattern of his life, says Lee, will risk loving one another without reservation and thus instinctively form a community to perpetuate Jesus' mission of preaching the kingdom.

Thus focused on the kingdom of God rather than on the perpetuation of their own institutional community, these model Christians would be a very effective instrument for promoting the collective power of good in this world. At the same time, they would not be obliged to give up their own special way of being a Christian in terms of their institutional history. Roman Catholics, for example, could still make use of seven sacraments rather than the two (baptism and Eucharist) to be found in many Protestant churches. Likewise, they could be governed by pope and bishops in the traditional manner. But their deeper allegiance would be to the kingdom of God and the collective power of good in this world, albeit in and through membership in the Roman Catholic Church. In similar fashion, the various Protestant denominations—with their strong emphasis on the preaching of the Word, a more modest sacramental system, and in many cases a different form of institutional governance—would be able to share with Roman Catholics in this common allegiance to the kingdom of God and the collective power of good in the world without danger to their historical institutional identity. Finally, the Eastern Orthodox churches would be free to contribute to the overall impact of the church on the building up of the kingdom of God in this world through their special focus on liturgy and contemplative prayer.

I make this claim, of course, based upon the field-oriented interpretation of Whiteheadian societies outlined above. If each of the Christian denominations represents a subfield of activity within the broader field of activity proper to Christianity as a whole, then each subfield can have its own pattern of existence and activity and yet contribute to the larger field of activity proper to Christianity as a whole. Within the human body, for example, there are many interrelated fields of activity, but in the end they all are integrated first into the field of activity proper to the brain and then to the field of activity proper to the mind or soul so as to constitute the unity of the human person. This is the key value of the notion of field. Unlike things or substances in the classical sense, fields can be incorporated into one another and influence one another's specific mode of operation without loss of individual identity or purpose. In fact, the more subfields of activity that can be incorporated into an overarching field of activity, the richer the pattern of existence and activity for the same overarching field of activity. The human being is a marvelous piece of genetic engineering, so to speak, because there is so much going on within the body/soul combination at the same time.

In more commonsense terms, Christianity is the richer because there are specifically different ways of being Christian as represented by the different Christian denominations. All Christians profess certain common beliefs and practice certain common rituals. This commonality of belief and ritual is enough to generate and hold in existence an overarching common field of activity for Christianity as a whole even as the subfields of activity proper to the different denominations differ from one another, sometimes rather markedly, in their patterns of governance and institutional life. In sacred Scripture, to be sure, Jesus predicts that someday there will be one flock and one shepherd (John 10:16). But he also says, "In my Father's house there are many mansions" (John 14:2), which would lead one to believe that there could be many different subgroups of sheep and their shepherds within that overall flock of which Jesus is the chief shepherd.

Similarly, non-Christian religious communities should also be able to contribute to the overarching reality of the kingdom of God. Not all of these groups, of course, would be comfortable with the expression "kingdom of God," but it would seem reasonable to suppose that all the major religions of the world could endorse the idea of contributing to the collective power of good and of resisting the harmful influence of the collective power of evil. All these religions, in virtue of their stated goals and values, encourage their members to strive for self-transcendence. Buddhism, for example, even though it classically prescinds from the question whether or not God exists, nevertheless preaches to its members the twin virtues of wisdom and compassion. Theravada Buddhism, practiced for the most part in Southeast Asia (e.g., Thailand, Cambodia, and Laos), emphasizes the wisdom of detachment from the self-centered needs and desires of the individual; Mahayana

Buddhism, as practiced chiefly in China, Korea, and Japan, stresses, on the contrary, compassion toward all sentient beings. Neither virtue is practiced apart from the other, and together they provide strong motivation for contributing to the collective power of good in this world as described above. Hence, why should not Buddhists be counted among those who help to build up what we Christians and other believers in God call the kingdom of God on earth?

Likewise, classical Chinese Confucianism lays heavy stress on the social virtues needed to live peacefully and harmoniously within various forms of community, beginning with the nuclear family but eventually embracing the entire universe. As Tu Wei-Ming comments, for Confucians the human self, "far from being an isolated individuality, is experientially and practically a center of relationships . . . It is through constant human interaction that we gradually learn to appropriate our selfhood as a transformative process. Indeed, our feelings, thoughts, and ideas are not necessarily our private properties. While they are intensely personal, they need not be private; they are often better thought of as shareable public goods."[4] While there is some question about whether heaven for Confucians is a personal God, there is no question that it is the privileged "source for moral creativity, meaning of life, and ultimate self-transformation."[5] Hence, the way of heaven for Confucians would seem to be practically identical with the kingdom of God for Christians and other believers in God.

Hence, it makes eminent good sense that non-Christian religions should add to the overall richness of the kingdom of God on earth even when they do not explicitly profess belief in God, still less belief in God as the Father of our Lord Jesus Christ. As Huston Smith, the celebrated author of *The World's Religions*, notes in the subtitle of his book, they together represent "Our Great Wisdom Traditions."[6] Insights into ultimate reality and our human relation to it which are barely mentioned or completely ignored in one tradition are the focal point of attention in another. As I tried to make clear in my earlier book *The Divine Matrix*,[7] for example, the Hindu notion of Brahman, the Buddhist understanding of emptiness or dependent co-origination, and Chinese reverence for the Tao that cannot be named should remind those of us who believe in a personal God (Christians, Jews, and Muslims) that there is a distinction between God as personal and the nonpersonal or transpersonal Godhead within our own traditions. The mystics in all three traditions testify to the mysterious character of the Godhead and to their own deep desire to be absorbed into the all-encompassing reality of the Godhead. Similarly, through extended dialogue with representatives of the various theistic religions, Hindus, Buddhists, Confucians, and Taoists may be led to a new appreciation of the latent interpersonal dimension of ultimate reality within their own religious traditions.

Of course, this is not to eliminate the legitimate diversity of the different world religions. The unity to be achieved among them in virtue of their mutual contribution to the collective power of good is not one of homogeneity or bland sameness. Rather it is a differentiated unity (curiously akin to the dynamic unity of the persons of the Trinity with one another) in which each religious group contributes its distinctive gifts and allows itself to be transformed through sharing in the special gifts of the other religious communities. Thus, the collective power of good in this world gains strength and the collective power of evil is held in check since valuable time and energy are not wasted by the members of the different religious communities trying to assert the intrinsic superiority of their tradition over all the others and thereby indirectly aiding that same collective power of evil. From a Christian Trinitarian perspective, moreover, what behavior could be more consonant with the image of God and with the likeness of Christ than the ongoing spontaneous gift of self to others and the grateful reception of the gift of self from others?

CHAPTER 6

"What is Truth?" (John 18:38)

P ILATE'S QUESTION to Jesus in John's Gospel that serves as
the title to this chapter has echoed down the ages and to
this day still has not been answered to everyone's satisfaction.
Is truth an ideal, something to be striven for but never quite
achieved? Or is it simply a fact provided that we have made a
correct judgment about the nature of reality? Does it reduce to
using the right research methods, or is it a matter of following
up on hunches? Scientists claim that they come close to the
truth about the physical world through employing a standard
method of hypothesis and verification. One studies the available data on a given subject, formulates a theory about how
things work or fit together, and comes back to the data to see
whether the theory explains the data. But scientists also admit
that they can never be sure that they are exactly right in their
theories. On principle, they keep looking for new evidence that
will either confirm the theory or make clear that it doesn't
work. For still other people, this is too complicated and time
consuming. One simply has to trust one's basic intuitions until
it becomes obvious that one has made a major mistake.

The great social reformer of India in the last century,
Mahatma Gandhi, dedicated his life to the pursuit of truth
(*satyagraha*) and eventually was murdered by one of his Hindu

compatriots because he acquiesced in the partition of India into two countries, the one predominately Hindu and the other basically Muslim. His single-minded pursuit of the truth thus eventually cost him his life. In less dramatic fashion, each of us is on a journey to the Truth: the truth of our own existence, the truth of our relationship to other human beings and the world of nature, and, above all, the truth of our relationship to God. But in the end do we ever really find the Truth or is the journey pointless? In brief, how do we know that our current understanding of the Truth is more or less on the mark and that we are not ultimately deceiving ourselves?

One of the great Roman Catholic theologians of the last half-century, Bernard Lonergan, S.J., claimed that truth and objectivity are inevitably the fruit of "authentic subjectivity."[1] There is much wisdom in this remark since we are all periodically guilty of self-deception. We simply do not want to accept what is staring us in the face and is evident to almost everyone else around us. Hence, being rigorously honest in our judgments about people and especially being properly self-critical in acknowledging our own deeper feelings and desires in each new situation, we unquestionably come closer to real objectivity in what we say and do. But is that enough? Are there forms of bias and prejudice of which we are truly unconscious but which have a very limiting effect on our ability to make objective judgments about people and new situations? Aren't racism and sexism, for example, frequently below the level of conscious awareness for many people?

The answer to this otherwise insuperable problem lies, in my judgment, in appeal to what we have already discussed at length in this book, namely, intersubjectivity. Our best chance for being truthful and objective in what we say and do is to be willing to share our thoughts and desires with other people and to listen to their response, to learn what they think and how they feel about the same issues. Through the give-and-take of dialogue with other people, we will gradually come to see the inevitable limits of our own customary perspective on life. In listening carefully to the views of other people, especially those who come from a different cultural background, we will come to recognize our unconscious biases and prejudices in a way that would be virtually impossible simply through extended self-reflection on our part.

But, you may object, are we not thereby just pooling our ignorance? If you are just as biased and prejudiced in your own way as I am, what chance do we have to arrive at truth and objectivity together? Those who have significant experience in dialogue with others, however, tell a different story. Dialogue works if you give it a real chance, if you do not become impatient at the lack of immediate results and break off the conversation in total exasperation. Real dialogue is hard work since it involves careful listening to the views of others, even when one is initially disinclined to accept what others are saying on the basis of their own experience. This does not mean that the others are right and that I am wrong on a given issue. It simply means that there will nearly always be a variety of standpoints on any important issue and that I can learn from attending to the views of others.

Sustained intersubjectivity, then, seems to be the normal context for growing in a sense of truth and objectivity on any given issue. If people continue in conversation with one another, they not only learn more about one another. They begin to learn from one another, to value the insights and perspectives of their partners in the dialogue. As a result, a new sense of common ground or shared perspectives begins to emerge. As this common ground becomes ever broader in scope, people instinctively feel that they are closer to the full truth and objectivity of the issue under discussion. If people of significantly different backgrounds basically agree on a given issue, then the likelihood that they are right grows proportionately. As we have seen in an earlier chapter, to be sure, communities as well as individuals are capable of self-deception with even more unfortunate consequences for everyone involved. But, if people in these communities are open to self-criticism about their communal policies and, above all, if they as members of one community are open to conversation with people from other communities on matters of common interest, then the likelihood of the group making a serious mistake in judgment is far less.

Basically this seems to have been what the American philosopher Josiah Royce had in mind with his notion of overlapping "communities of interpretation," which ultimately converge in a single Universal Community of Interpretation embracing all humankind.[2] Individual human beings come to knowledge of the truth through interpreting signs of various kinds (words, gestures, actions) from one another.[3] A sign by definition is always the manifestation or expression of the mind of an individual or a group. I understand the mind of another person when I properly interpret the signs which he or she is offering me. But, in order to be sure that I understand these signs, I have to stay in touch with that other person through signs (words, gestures, actions) of my own. Thus, for interpretation to work, there must be a community of minds, a group of people who continuously offer interpretations to one another of their words, gestures, and actions toward one another.[4] All these overlapping communities of interpretation then converge to form the Universal Community, which corresponds to the kingdom of God on earth.[5]

Royce imaged God as the Supreme Interpreter within the Universal Community who "interprets all to all, and each individual to the world, and the world of spirits to each individual."[6] But within my own model of God as a community of divine persons actively engaged with their creatures in bringing about the kingdom of God on earth, the notion of a Universal Community of Interpretation can be expanded to include the divine persons as the founding or original members of that same community. The divine persons, after all, are one God rather than three gods in close collaboration because they share so completely the experience of being God with one another. Each is God in a different way or from a different perspective. The "Father" is God in virtue of being the Eternal Source of the divine being; the "Son" is God in virtue of being the Eternal Respondent to the Father's gift of Self; the "Spirit" is God in virtue of being the Eternal Mediator or Principle of Unity between the Father and the Son. Yet, in deeply sharing with one another these different ways of being God, they are together the full reality of God, a perfect "community of interpretation."

Furthermore, in their activity on behalf of us, their creatures, they extend their own divine community of interpretation into the world of creation. They offer to us "signs" of their presence and activity in our midst for us to interpret and act upon. The world of Nature in all its complexity is one such sign. Sacred Scripture is still another even more complex sign of the presence and activity of the divine persons among us. From the book of Genesis to the Apocalypse or book of Revelation, we have at our disposal a chronicle of God's dealings first with the people of Israel and then with the early Christian communities. Initially the Hebrew Prophets were inspired by God to offer their interpretation of these signs of God's presence in their midst. Then, within the Gospel narratives Jesus is presented as interpreting the "signs of the times" in the light of his reading of the Hebrew Bible and his ongoing internal communication with the Father and the Spirit. Finally, Paul and the other New Testament writers continued the work of Jesus in interpreting for the communities entrusted to them the signs of God's presence and activity in their midst.

Yet, you may object, truth has to do with facts, not simply with human understanding or interpretation of those facts. Objective reality is "out there," independently of our paying attention to it or trying to change it. On a personal level, this has to be true. As the old saying goes, wishing something were not the case doesn't make it so. But, on the group level, it is frequently a different story. When a group of urban planners, for example, see some farmland outside a metropolitan area as a desirable place to live, they can make it happen. With proper funding and advertising, they can convert that thinly populated farmland into a new suburb with row after row of houses linked by gently curving streets and with a shopping center right in the middle. So "objective reality" is seldom, if ever, absolutely fixed and unchanging. It keeps changing, depending in no small measure upon how people relate to it and make decisions about it.

To put this issue of objective reality in an even broader context, we can call to our aid once again the philosophy of Alfred North Whitehead. Whitehead claimed that "the final real things of which the world is made up" are actual occasions or momentary self-constituting subjects of experience.[7] When an actual occasion is in process of self-constitution, it "prehends" or on a feeling level draws into itself data from the world around it. In coming to a decision as to how to relate to all this information from the outside world, it has to sort out or interpret for itself what it all means. Then, when it has thus come to a decision about its own reality, its own place in the world around it, it communicates or shares itself with all later actual occasions or subjects of experience for them to "prehend" as part of their own self-constitution.[8] Likewise, when a series of such actual occasions coalesces to form what Whitehead calls a "society," they end up constituting a joint field of activity with an objective pattern or structure. Finally, all these structured fields of activity, from the simplest to the most complex, make up what you and I on the commonsense level of experience call reality: the people and things (both living and nonliving) in the world around us.

So for Whitehead objective reality is what it is only because a virtually infinite number of actual occasions or momentary subjects of experience are constantly interpreting the world around them and passing on to their successors the patterns or structures proper both to their individual constitution and to the societies or fields of activity into which they aggregate. The whole world is thus an ongoing process of interpretation or a Universal Community of Interpretation such as Josiah Royce envisioned.[9] Objective reality as something apart from subjects of experience who are interpreting it for themselves and thereby subtly changing it for their successors simply does not exist.

Once again you may call a halt and say: "Okay, an interesting theory. But so what? What difference does it make to you and to me in terms of the way we practically live our lives here and now?" As I see it, basic acceptance of this approach to truth and objectivity could make an enormous difference in the way we relate to other people, above all, in those situations where we find ourselves at odds with one another over what is right and wrong, over what is true and false. The search for truth, the passion for settling what is right and wrong here and now, can divide us as well as unite us. Everything depends upon how we relate to people with whom we disagree. If we are so convinced that we are right that we are willing to use force of one kind or another to get our way, then the search for truth will tear us apart, divide us into warring factions who deeply dislike and distrust one another. If, on the contrary, we are persuaded that mutual dialogue rather than force is the appropriate strategy in conflict situations, then the search for truth will slowly bring us together, allow us to grow in respect and trust for one another. In brief, the quest for truth is a two-edged sword. It can wound or it can heal, depending upon how we go about it. Finding a satisfactory answer to the question "What is truth?" therefore, is not idle speculation but a useful tool for dealing with other people in conflict situations. Let us see then how this theory would work out in practice.

First, even though truth is in process of development, this does not mean that the world is completely different from moment to moment and that our understanding of ourselves and of the world in which we live is purely haphazard. Even though each moment of consciousness represents for us a new world in terms of what is currently going on around us and our own response to it, the differences from the world of a moment ago are usually very minor. Only over time do these subtle differences in perspective add up so as to constitute a really significant change in our understanding of ourselves and the world in which we live. Hence, there are enduring truths even if not strictly speaking eternal truths to be found in this world. Furthermore, for Christians who believe in the doctrine of the Trinity there is always the one great truth which is the unvarying structure of their relationship to the three divine persons. For these Christians the ultimate truth of their own existence and activity is anchored in their participation in the divine life, sharing in the ongoing dialogue between the Father, the Son, and the Holy Spirit. Everything else in their lives can undergo gradual modification provided this unique set of relationships remains the same and transforms their existence in all its various details.

Second, by urging that truth is thus radically intersubjective or communitarian, I not only mean that there are many individual human beings together seeking the truth (as in Royce's Universal Community of Interpretation). I also think that each of us possesses the truth to the extent that we participate (consciously or unconsciously) in the worldwide community of truth-seekers. Each of us finds our truth, the truth of our own existence and activity, in the truth proper to the world around us but only as a partial reflection of that same truth. Recall what I said above about an actual occasion or momentary subject of experience as an interpreter of the world around it and as a sign for subsequent actual occasions to prehend or internalize for their own self-constitution. Each actual occasion is therefore a microcosm of the world around it from its own limited perspective, and its truth here and now is a truth proper to that world as well as to itself. By definition it cannot express the whole truth about the world in which it lives, but the truth which it does express in virtue of its own self-constitution is necessarily its truthful interpretation of the world in which it exists.

The irony of our human condition, of course, is that, while we are conscious of ourselves as truth-seekers, we often fail to understand this communitarian dimension of truth. That is, we fail to see that the truth about the world which we prehend from moment to moment and the truth of our own existence as a result is only a limited reflection of the full truth or the truth of the world as a whole. Moreover, in our eagerness to communicate to others our own version of the truth we fail to see that our mission in life as truth-seekers is to contribute to a reality greater than ourselves of which we will never be fully cognizant. Quite the contrary, we tend to substitute our own subjective understanding of the truth (which is true enough in terms of our own experience) for objective truth, that which is true even apart from our own (or anyone else's) experience. Yet no such objective truth exists. All truth is the expression of someone's subjective experience of reality and contributes to the formation of a new objective reality, which will be open to interpretation by a new set of truth-seekers, a new set of actual occasions or momentary subjects of experience consciously or unconsciously in search of the truth.

Once again, however, what about factual truth, that which is simply the case here and now? If every actual occasion or momentary subject of experience is a microcosm of the world around it, then the truth which it expresses in virtue of its own self-constitution is indeed factual. It is a de facto reflection of the world as it existed a moment ago and a constitutive factor in the new reality of that bigger world coming into being at this moment. Factual truth is thus present in an individual human being's experience of truth provided that it is not mis-interpreted, provided that it is not simply mistaken for objective truth. On the contrary, we fallible human beings would be far better advised to deepen and enrich our own subjective understanding of the truth of any given issue by comparing it with the truth experiences of other individuals on the same subject. In this way, without denying the value of our own experience (which is, after all, our only access to the truth) we will inevitably relativize our own truth claims with respect to the rival truth claims of other individuals. Thus by degrees we will come to an appreciation, even if not a comprehensive understanding, of the process whereby truth is acquired and reality is changed from moment to moment.

Yet isn't truth somehow lost in the confusion of different standpoints on the truth? No; as already mentioned, through sustained dialogue among truth-seekers there should emerge by degrees a convergence of standpoints on a given theme or subject matter so that these different standpoints form an interconnected whole, the equivalent of a consensus position. A consensus position, of course, is not the same as a universal standpoint. While a universal standpoint by definition prescinds from particular standpoints in order to serve as the norm of objectivity for all the others, a consensus position arises out of the dynamic interrelation of all the particular standpoints on a given issue and will inevitably reflect residual disagreements as well as a growing sense of agreement among the individuals representing those same standpoints. The unanimity that we human beings thereby achieve is then not the unanimity of a single comprehensive standpoint to which all of us must submit because it alone represents what is in fact the case. Rather, it is the unanimity achieved through our mutual recognition of interconnected partial standpoints, all of which contain some truth but none of which contains the whole truth.

When we engage in dialogue with other people, then, we should start by mentally acknowledging the possible interconnectedness of all the different standpoints to be thus represented. This will help us to put in context the claims to objective truth that will subsequently be made in the course of the dialogue (beginning, of course, with our own truth claims). We should also mentally prepare ourselves for the possibility of residual disagreements in our dealings with one another. Residual disagreements, after all, only indicate that the dialogue needs to be continued for the indefinite future. Truth-seeking is an ongoing process. Settling for half-truths along the way only impedes the process of coming to the full truth, or in any case a greater truth.

Let us put all this in the specific context of interreligious dialogue, dialogue among the adherents of the various world religions. Real progress will be made here only if the participants recognize not only the relative character of the truth claims of other religions but also the relative character of the truth claims of their own religion. This is not to say that the truth claims proper to one's own religion are false or untrue, but only that they do not represent the whole truth about ultimate reality, whether ultimate reality be conceived as a personal God or as an impersonal cosmic force. Participants to interreligious dialogue thus have much to learn from one another. In the process of sustained dialogue with one another, they will learn much about the truth claims of other religions from those who actively practice those religions, but they will learn even more about the truth claims of their own religion. In coming to understand and appreciate the truth experiences of non-Christians, Christians will come to understand and appreciate on a much deeper level the truth claims of Christianity. This is how they will concretely experience the truth of their own religion as both in process and radically interpersonal. Truth is our most precious possession, but it will remain such a treasure only if we share it first with our Christian brothers and sisters, and ultimately with all humankind.

CHAPTER 7

Divine Providence and Human Freedom

IF YOU OR I were asked whether we believe that we are free to make our own decisions, presumably we would say yes without hesitation. Likewise, if we were asked whether God is in control of the world and is taking care of us personally, we would also normally say yes. But is there an implicit contradiction here? Can we human beings, both individually and collectively, be in charge of our lives at the same time that God is in charge of human history and the world of nature? Does my freedom somehow limit the freedom of the divine persons to achieve their goals in creation and, vice versa, does their providence over this world somehow predetermine what will happen to me both now and at every future moment of my life? Perhaps the answer to these questions lies in a better understanding of the relationship between time and eternity. The three divine persons living in eternity are not limited by the conditions of space and time as we are. They see the bigger picture and make decisions about us and our contemporaries that help us and allow them to stay in control of the world. But what happens when what they want for us and what we want for ourselves are not the same? Who wins in the case of a standoff?

The only honest answer to these questions is to admit that we really don't know if only because we do not understand time all that well, much less eternity. As St. Augustine famously remarked in his *Confessions*, he felt that he understood time until someone asked him about it, and then he realized that he was no longer sure what it was.[1] In the end, he seemed to have thought of time primarily in terms of the present since in his mind the past no longer exists and the future does not exist yet. But he also conceded that the present is never the same from moment to moment since, if it remained always the same, it would be identical with eternity.[2] As Lawrence Fagg points out, what Augustine was actually describing was our human experience of time as something that flows out of the future into the present and from there into the past. What he did not take into account, however, was time as measured in his day by a sundial or in our age by a clock: namely, time as that which flows in the reverse direction from the past into the present and thence into the future.[3]

Even more problems arise when we try to think about eternity. Do we see eternity, for example, as the opposite of time—namely, as timeless without any sense of movement or flow? Or do we with Whitehead see eternity as unending time, a sequence of moments without any beginning or end?[4] Is eternity thus simply an indefinite extension of our own human experience of time; or, on the contrary, is time, as the ancient philosopher Plato commented in *Timaeus*, the "moving image of eternity," the imperfect representation of something completely beyond our comprehension?[5]

For me the most satisfying explanation of the relationship between time and eternity is to say that eternity is "the togetherness of past, present, and future." My guide here is Robert Neville in his book *Eternity and Time's Flow*.[6] Neville argues that we simultaneously live both in time and in eternity and that eternity is always in the background whenever we become aware of the passage of time. While I agree with him on this point, I also think that this same approach to time and eternity helps us understand how the three divine persons can simultaneously be in eternity and be assisting us here in time at the same "time." Thinking of time and eternity as interconnected, we possibly have a better chance of reconciling divine providence and human freedom. Likewise, knowing how the divine persons are at work in our lives, we should be in a better position to take advantage of their assistance when we especially need it, in time of crisis.

When Neville proposes that eternity is the togetherness of past, present, and future, he does not simply mean that there is always a before and after for each moment of time: one thing after another without interruption. The deeper togetherness of past, present, and future is that they are necessarily interrelated and interdependent. Thus they keep changing with every new event: "Not only is something new always happening— the present is steadily moving on to new dates—but the past is always growing and the structure of future possibilities is constantly shifting in response to the decisions made in each moment of present actualization."[7] The present, in other words, is indeed the moment of decision here and now but each such decision changes both the past and the future. Something new has been added to the past so that it is not remembered in quite the same way as before the decision. Likewise, the present decision reshapes the future because now I have to take into account what I just decided in looking ahead to the future.

For example, see what happens when two people decide to get married. As soon as they make that decision, both the past and the future are different for each of them. That is, they will each look back upon their individual past lives as somehow leading up first to their getting acquainted, then to falling in love and deciding to get married. Likewise, from this time forward they will be facing the future as a couple, sharing the ups and downs of life together. So not only is the present decision to get married added to the sum total of their past decisions, but it reconfigures the meaning and value of all the other past decisions. Similarly, the present decision will set in motion a new set of decisions for them. The couple will have to start planning for their joint future in a way that they would not have done up to that point.

Admittedly, the decision to get married is one of the biggest decisions one will ever make and has as a result an extraordinary impact on one's sense of the past and future. Other decisions as a result are far less dramatic, and the impact on one's past and future far less obvious. But Neville's basic point is that time is not to be represented as a sequence of individual moments like so many ticks on a clock, each with its own separate identity. Rather, time is an organic unity with its parts or members (past, present, and future) in ongoing dynamic interrelation. None of these time dimensions can exist by itself apart from the other two. The past, after all, has no significance except as the necessary context for a decision in the present which in turn will affect the future. Likewise, the future as the world of possibilities for decisions in the present is inevitably restricted by decisions made in the past. If I change jobs, for example, then I normally have to make still other changes in my customary way of life.

Consider also how our sense of time changes as we progressively move through life. For example, when we are young, the future looms large. But when we are old, the past figures more importantly in our decision making. Each of us has our own time system that subtly changes character with the passage of time. Time is also a factor for everyone and everything else in the world around us. There seem to be so many different time systems, some bigger than others, some longer in duration than others. The life span of an insect is minuscule by comparison with the life span of a human being, but the life span of a human being is in turn dwarfed by the temporal duration of a redwood tree in the Pacific Northwest. Even inanimate things exist in time, and the societies of actual occasions or momentary subjects of experience making them up must also have some limited experience of the passage of time. The Rocky Mountains in the United States or the Alps in Western Europe, for example, have slowly taken shape over thousands of years and endure to the present day. How should we picture the passage of time for the societies of actual occasions making up these mountain ranges? Finally, on the presupposition that the universe itself is a vast interconnected totality, an all-encompassing time system composed of innumerable subsystems, then it too has its own past, present, and projected future which only a Creator God can comprehend and thus in some way direct or guide along certain lines rather than others.

Thus we are brought back to the notion of divine providence, both in our own lives and in the universe around us. How does divine providence somehow regulate and coordinate all these differing time systems? Recall, first of all, the concept of eternity as the togetherness of past, present, and future. Presumably for the three divine persons, eternity is also the togetherness of past, present, and future. But their past necessarily overlaps the past for each of us as individuals, the past of all other human beings, even the past of the entire universe from the Big Bang onwards. The past of the divine persons is the past history of the divine life, which may have included still other universes that in the meantime have come and gone. By the same token, the present for the three divine persons includes not only all the events taking place in our universe but also events possibly taking place in other universes existing simultaneously with ours but with which we have as yet no contact. Finally, the future for the divine persons extends well beyond the time that our universe, at least in its present form, will cease to exist.

But, perhaps most importantly, eternity as the togetherness of past, present, and future should likewise be an ever-changing interconnected reality for the divine persons, just as it is for each of us. The three divine persons, in other words, do not exist in a timeless "now" where past, present, and future stand still and can be viewed by the divine persons as a single determinate reality.[8] Rather, while the basic structure of their internal relationships to one another remains unchanged, specific details of the past, present, and future for the divine persons are continually reconfigured in view of their ongoing involvement in our world and perhaps in other worlds as well. Thomas Aquinas argues in the *Summa Theologiae* that God is present to events in this world as they happen, in their "presentiality."[9] But in its presentiality every created event is likewise linked with its past as the realm of stubborn fact and with its future as the realm of logical possibility. Hence, whether the divine persons focus on individual events taking place in this world at every moment or on the cosmic process as a whole from the Big Bang onwards, their knowledge of us and our world is never timeless, a fixed reality, but always in process of development toward the future. That future is in the first place the future of the divine life, but also the future of our world and of any other world existing as a vital part of that same divine life.

Yet one must still ask what role the divine persons play in this ongoing cosmic drama. Presumably, they are not just silent spectators, helpless to influence what they see happening in our world. How do they get involved without interfering with the spontaneity of their creatures, without compromising human free choice? I believe that they are involved with us in terms of what Aristotle and Thomas Aquinas called efficient and final causality.

Efficient causality is the power to make things happen; I decide to get out of bed in the morning and in due time I am on my feet and ready to start the day. Final causality is the power to give order and direction to what I have just decided to do; after getting out of bed, I start thinking about all the things that I have to do that day, beginning with breakfast. The divine persons likewise employ efficient and final causality with respect to creation, but they do so in a manner exactly opposite to the way in which we human beings and all the other creatures of this world exercise efficient and final causality on our own behalf.

The divine persons make things happen by giving us "initial aims," by enabling us to be ourselves at every moment. This is a minimal exercise of efficient causality on their part since in the end the decision is ours, not theirs. But they are much more active in terms of final causality. The divine initial aim, after all, not only empowers us to make a decision but is likewise a feeling-level lure or sense of direction and purpose for us in making that decision. Because they see the bigger picture for each of us as individuals and for our world at any given moment, the divine persons are in a unique position to guide us to a better rather than a worse decision at every moment of our lives.

How does that contrast with the way in which we human beings and other creatures exercise efficient and final causality? In making our own decisions with the help of the divine initial aim, we are a lot more responsible than the divine persons at any given moment. We more than they make things happen. Yet our vision of what sort of decision to make is always very limited; we cannot realistically foresee the consequences of any given decision beyond the immediate future. Hence, we need the directionality contained within the divine initial aim in making our decisions from moment to moment. Thus in terms of final causality the divine persons, not we ourselves, play the greater role. Provided that we are responsive to the divine lure as it is presented to us moment by moment, we can be reasonably confident that there is indeed a sense of purpose and direction to our lives that transcends the goals and values which we might perceive at any given moment.

So the divine persons exercise providence over our individual lives and over the direction of the cosmic process as a whole, but they do it indirectly through the provision of divine initial aims with which we must cooperate if we are to gain a stronger sense of purpose and direction in our lives. Contrast this with the traditional understanding of divine providence that emphasizes much more strongly God's unilateral activity in the world of creation. As transcendent First Efficient Cause, God creates or brings into being everything that happens in this world. But this means that everything that happens is such only because God somehow wills it to happen one way rather than some other way. As Thomas Aquinas notes, there is nothing in the creature which does not come from God since God is the cause of its total being.[10] Hence, the creature is not primarily responsible for what happens since it is God who brings it into being and sustains it in existence. Similarly, as Ultimate Final Cause God orders everything without exception to its final end as part of the divine plan for the salvation of the world. Very little seems to be left for us human beings to do in terms of either efficient or final causality.

Here one might object that this is a caricature of what must be the case. It is obvious that we make plans and do things on our own; God does not do everything for us. I totally agree. The problem lies with the classical explanation of how this happens. Aquinas and other classically oriented theologians put so much emphasis on God's unilateral activity in the world that there is little or no room left for our response. My own approach is to indicate how we share efficient and final causality with the divine persons. We creatures exercise most of the efficient causality; we make things happen in this world by our own independent decisions. The divine persons exercise most of the final causality. They do most of the planning both for our own future as individuals and for the future of the world as a whole.

The three divine persons, in other words, are primarily at work in the lives of us human beings and other creatures by providing information to guide our decisions at every moment and thereby indirectly to steer human history and the entire cosmic process over time in one direction rather than in another. This requires infinite patience on their part since we creatures do not always respond to the divine initial aim as we should, and bad things happen as a result. But, as a matter of fact, is this not what we see when we review the up-and-down character of human history and the meandering way in which evolution has proceeded on this earth? There is evidently no exact blueprint for what happens in this world, yet everything is not thereby left to chance. There still seems to be an underlying divine purpose or directionality both to human history and to cosmic evolution.

Yet here one may say: "Okay, you win the argument with the Thomists. So what difference does it make? What is the 'cash value' of your theory in terms of day-to-day life as a Christian?"

First of all, we should not blame the divine persons if things are not going so well for us in the here and now. The primary responsibility for what happens from moment to moment lies with ourselves and the people around us. Our predecessors in this world got us into this mess, at least to some extent. But here and now we are responsible for what happens next; we are the authors of our own decisions, whether for better or for worse. At the same time, we should not be too hard on ourselves and our predecessors. Much that happens is not anyone's fault. Since the divine persons have given us and other creatures so much freedom of choice, we should expect things to go wrong periodically. But even so, the real question is still what to do when things go wrong.

Here I turn to Rabbi Harold Kushner, who wrote a celebrated book on this topic, *When Bad Things Happen to Good People*. His advice, in brief, was not to complain to God that things have gone wrong without fault on one's part, nor to ask God to work a miracle on one's behalf, but, much more importantly, to seek God's assistance in deciding what to do next.[11] Kushner came to this conclusion not on the basis of some philosophical argument such as I have proposed above, but in virtue of a great tragedy in his personal and family life. He and his wife, both devout Jews, had a child with Progeria (rapid aging) Syndrome, which meant that the child would age many times faster than normal and die of old age generally as a teenager. Like Job in the Hebrew Bible, he and his wife had every reason to complain that they had done nothing wrong to deserve this affliction. Nor did physicians hold out any reasonable hope for the child's unexpected recovery from the disease. In the end, all that they could do was to seek divine assistance in deciding how to cope with this tragedy. Over time Kushner realized that precisely in this way God was at work in his life. In humbly seeking God's assistance in their time of sorrow, he and his wife gained both strength and wisdom to deal with their pain and sense of loss.

In my judgment, this is where theory and practice reinforce one another. The theory, such as I have presented it above, allows one peacefully to surrender cherished illusions about divine omnipotence, what God can do in this world if God wants, and to accept with equanimity the notion that God's power in dealing with us is more in terms of persuasion than coercion. This is not to deny the logical possibility God could work a miracle, something unexplainable by conventional human reasoning, since such events do seem to occur at rare intervals. But the normal pattern of divine activity in the world seems to be that of urging creatures to make the more sensible decision, to take the more prudent course of action in a given set of circumstances. Then, if the course of events turns out badly for whatever reason, God is once again active in assisting human beings (and within limits nonhuman creatures as well), providing them with a feeling-level lure or felt sense of direction for the decision of the next moment in dealing with a bad situation that can no longer be averted.

For human beings, then, prayer in time of need should be far more a humble request for divine assistance in dealing with difficult situations than a impassioned plea that God do something dramatic to change the situation. As Jesus commented in teaching his disciples how to pray, "Your Father knows what you need before you ask him" (Matt. 6:8). Accordingly, he urged them to be open in prayer to what the Father wants for them here and now and to ask for the grace to follow through on the Father's prompting (or in Whiteheadian terms, the Father's initial aims).

Naturally, given the customary babble of "voices" that each of us hears when we turn inward to make a decision, it is not always easy to discern the lure or felt impulse of the Father from other urgings coming out of our own past history and previous contacts with other people. But, as already noted in an earlier chapter, Jesus himself in his human consciousness developed the habit of listening for the Father's voice, above all, in moments of crisis or decision during his public life. Likewise, other masters of the spiritual life like St. Ignatius Loyola have set down rules for "the discernment of spirits" to assist those making progress in the spiritual life.[12] So attending to the divine initial aims is not an impossible task, but only one which requires time and patience on the part of the individual seeking God's will for himself or herself.

Prayer for others with their special needs, of course, is another case altogether. Presumably we do not have to persuade the three divine persons to be attentive to the needs of our relatives and friends. In their ongoing providence for all their creatures, the divine persons are fully aware of each new situation as it develops. What is the point then of offering prayers for the intentions of others in the expectation that God will somehow intervene to avert something painful for them or, on the contrary, to bring about some great good for them? The answer to this question is developed in the next chapter.

CHAPTER 8

Prayer and the Collective Power of Good

"IF PRAYER WORKED the way many people think it does, no one would ever die, because no prayer is ever offered more sincerely than the prayer for life, for health and recovery from illness, for ourselves and for those we love."[1] With this reminder about the inevitable ups and downs of life in this world, Rabbi Harold Kushner begins an extended reflection on what happens when prayer is apparently not answered and we are left wondering whether prayer either for our own needs or for the needs of others is not ultimately a futile exercise, a waste of time and energy. His answer is twofold. Prayer for one's own needs and desires should not be too specific. We should not expect, in other words, that God will work a miracle in order to give us what we want here and now:

> People who pray for miracles usually don't get miracles, any more than children who pray for bicycles, good grades, or boyfriends get them as a result of praying. But people who pray for courage, for strength to bear the unbearable, for the grace to remember what they have left instead of what they have lost, very often find their prayers answered. They discover that they have more strength, more courage than they ever knew themselves to have.[2]

This approach resonates nicely with Whitehead's notion of divine initial aims, which we discussed in the last chapter. God is ever present to assist us in the changing circumstances of our lives, but ultimately we must learn to follow God's lead in making our moment-by-moment decisions. We must trust that God understands our current problems far better than we do and that through the initial aim God is offering us a practical way to cope with those same problems. In the short run, of course, the divine initial aim may be more painful than pleasurable as when God keeps gently urging a drug addict to seek outside help for his or her chemical dependency. But in the long run it will be seen as the best possible choice one could have made under the circumstances.

The other response put forth by Kushner to the problem of unanswered prayer has to do with prayer for and with others, such as people offer at a religious service together with other members of the congregation. "Prayer, when it is offered in the right way, redeems people from isolation. It assures them that they need not feel alone and abandoned. It lets them know that they are part of a greater reality, with more depth, more hope, more courage, and more of a future than any individual could have by himself."[3] As I see it, what Kushner is alluding to here is what I have called the collective power of good (or in more specifically religious terms the kingdom of God). The collective power of good is that greater reality to which we all, at least in our better moments, contribute and which, if trustingly embraced, will surely endow our prayers for others with an efficacy beyond anything we could imagine simply as private individuals here and now.

But, practically speaking, how do we tap into the collective power of good in offering prayers for others? One obvious way is through participating in the sacramental rituals of the church. The sacraments bring us together as a community and allow us to pray for ourselves and all those present in the congregation, but also to pray for relatives and friends not present and for the needs of the church and the world. When the liturgy "works," we leave church feeling comforted and strengthened for living the Christian life more fully. Keeping this in mind, let us now focus on the two sacraments recognized by all Christians: baptism and Eucharist. In addition, I offer some reflections on marriage as a sacramental sign of God's love for us and our love both for God and for one another. My guide here will be Bernard Cooke in his classic work *Sacraments and Sacramentality*.[4]

Cooke believes that all of life is sacramental. All of life speaks to us of the loving presence of God if we are prepared properly to interpret what is happening to us.[5] But this is not always easy to do. We need what Cooke calls a "hermeneutic of experience," mental guidelines that equip us to interpret our experience in a more accurate and profound way.[6] One such hermeneutic of experience for Christians is to be found in the Bible as the revealed Word of God, but another hermeneutic is the sacramental system of the church. Sacraments structure the Christian life and give it meaning and value. Likewise, sacraments allow us to pray together for our common needs and thereby to contribute in a more significant way to the collective power of good in the world.

With reference to baptism, Cooke reminds us that Christianity is not unique in having initiation rites; even purely secular organizations have specific initiation rites.[7] But for Christians and members of other world religions, initiation does not end with the celebration of a ritual but is a lifelong process whereby one slowly conforms one's individual self-identity to the self-identity of the group, its enduring goals and values.[8] Unfortunately within Western Christianity this notion of baptism as the start of an ongoing process of conversion became obscured because the focus of the sacrament shifted in the early centuries from adult baptism to infant baptism. Parents were anxious to have their infant children baptized so as to guard against the danger of the child dying prematurely without being baptized. Since Vatican II, however, the Roman Catholic Church has given new attention to adult baptism and the catechumenate as the necessary period of instruction and discernment before receiving the sacrament. This new rite draws attention to "the understandings, attitudes, intentions, and hopes of the person being baptized, as well as of the community receiving him or her into its midst."[9]

But what are those attitudes and intentions which the newly baptized person shares with the Christian community at large? The first is a vision of what it means to be human based upon the life, teachings, death, and resurrection of Jesus. In Jesus a new humanity has come into being, a new creation is in progress, a new and definitive phase of the kingdom of God has been inaugurated.[10] The second is a sense of responsibility for sharing this vision: "To be a Christian is to be a disciple, to join with the risen Christ in his continuing work of bringing into being the kingdom of God, which is the ultimate well-being of humans."[11] Third, as part of the baptismal liturgy, one renounces Satan and all his works and pomps. What does this mean but that one promises to set aside many of the self-centered values of contemporary culture in order to implement the more self-giving values enunciated by Jesus in his Sermon on the Mount? Fourth, one shares with others the conviction that being a Christian is the most important feature of one's life. Finally, with Christ and with one's fellow Christians one shares the gift of the Holy Spirit, the sustaining presence of the triune God at every moment and in every decision.

Although baptism is received only once, Eucharist is celebrated weekly, if not daily. Eucharist is thus the key to sustaining and deepening one's baptismal promises in company with others who have made the same commitments. As Cooke comments, "The immediate disciples of Jesus gathered in small groups to recall what Jesus had said and done, to attempt some interpretation of his death and resurrection that would fit into their story of God's dealings with humans, and to make present through eucharistic commemoration the abiding presence of this risen Lord."[12] This is likewise what we Christians still do at the present time when we assemble in churches to celebrate the Eucharist. We listen to the Gospel narratives and other readings out of the Old and New Testament in order to remind ourselves one more time what Jesus said and did. Then with the homily of the priest or minister as a guide, we apply the teachings of Scripture to our own lives in various ways. Finally, with minds and hearts prepared, we offer our lives to "God the Father" under the symbols of bread and wine and receive in communion those same symbols of bread and wine as the consecrated Body and Blood of the risen Lord. Furthermore, we do all this together as a Eucharistic community, as a group of people seeking to live out their baptismal commitments.

The eucharistic ritual has in many ways remained unchanged for the two thousand years of the church's existence. What has changed, as Cooke astutely notes, is the realization by Christians of what they are up against in terms of living out the Christian way of life, in consciously deciding to be a disciple of Jesus in today's world. In renouncing Satan with all his works and pomps, Christians find themselves today confronting evil in largely systemic terms: "Obviously, it is human beings who do evil, but because of the complication and vast organization of life today, much of the evil that afflicts people happens through the vast and impersonal systems that are so much a part of modern life."[13] This systemic evil or what I have called the collective power of evil is what Christians, both as individuals and above all as a community, must resist in order to guarantee for themselves and others their status as free and responsible human beings in the face of mounting social pressure and even overt physical violence. Here is where prayer not only for oneself and one's own needs but also prayer for others with their needs takes on new urgency. Christians gather weekly or even daily to offer common prayer for the needs of the church and contemporary society.

But how do we know that it works, that it does any good to pray for someone else in his or her need? First of all, we have the example of Jesus during his earthly life. Jesus was clearly aware of the systemic character of evil, the power of evil as something suprahuman or demonic. He was always ready to forgive individual sinners, but he was unyielding in his opposition to the social evils of his day and quite pointed in his criticism of those like the Scribes and Pharisees who supported an unjust social order because they themselves stood to gain by it. Even more importantly, however, he recruited a band of disciples to assist him in preaching the nearness of the kingdom of God, a new social order based on the fundamental equality of all human beings before their Creator God. Jesus evidently believed then that in conscious opposition to the collective power of evil in the world there can and should exist a collective power of good, communities of men and women united in their opposition to the manifest social evils of the day.

We show our united opposition to the collective power of evil in openly praying with others for our common needs. Our common prayer is effective because it somehow releases positive energy, the power of love, into the world which God (or, in specifically Christian terms, the triune God) can tailor to fit the needs of specific people in specific situations. It may seem strange to think of love in purely physical terms as a form of energy, but we all know that love is a powerful factor in human relations. It emboldens us to say and do things that we would hesitate to do simply on our own. Why should it not then be considered as a form of energy ultimately derived from the divine communitarian life, the ongoing exchange of life and love among the three divine persons? If so, then through our prayers for others the divine persons can make use of a new source of positive energy for enhancing the collective power of good in this world here and now. In interpersonal relations, after all, one plus one often equals three, not just two. The power of love grows with the union of minds and hearts.

Yet one must be realistic here. The power of God's love works through persuasion, not coercion. Even with the help of our prayers for others, initial aims from the divine persons do not overpower the free will of human beings, but only persuade and inspire them to move in a certain direction. Hence, prayer for others and their needs will not in every case be judged by us as totally successful, at least in the short term. But, according to the teachings of Jesus (e.g., Matt. 7:7–11; Mark 11:23; Luke 11:9–13), prayer is always answered, even if the results of the power of prayer are humanly perceived only in the long run. We have to trust that our prayer for others will be effective, especially if it is combined with the prayer of Christians around the world for the same ends.

Is it impossible then to pray for others simply on one's own and without reference to the prayer of the church? Since Christians are urged to pray always whenever opportunity provides, it is clear that one can pray effectively even apart from direct participation in formal church services. To take a cue from the Liturgy of the Hours or the Divine Office recited by priests, religious, and some laypeople every day, even when one is praying alone one is still praying in union with other Christians around the world. The person praying the Breviary, in other words, is implicitly linking his or her prayer with the prayer of other Christians around the world as they together offer to God this prayer which originated with medieval monks chanting the Divine Office together in the monastery chapel. The efficacy of such prayer is that it gives glory to God but, even more importantly, that it contributes to the collective power of good at work in this world. It may immediately be directed to the needs of particular individuals, but in the end it is offered to God for the needs of the whole Christian community around the world and, for that matter, for the needs of humankind as a whole. The collective power of good is not restricted to Christians but in the end includes all those who seek to live lives of service and self-giving love to others. Only together, in union of minds and hearts, will good people be able effectively to resist the all-pervasive influence of the collective power of evil in this world.

Another dimension of the Eucharist which perhaps has been more stressed in Roman Catholic than in Protestant circles is the doctrine of the Real Presence, namely, that in virtue of the words of consecration at the Eucharistic liturgy Jesus is really present to the faithful under the symbols of bread and wine and remains there even after the Eucharistic service is finished. Historically, the Roman Catholic Church has explained this belief in terms of the doctrine of transubstantiation, namely, that in virtue of the words of consecration at the Eucharistic liturgy the substance of the bread and the wine is converted into the substance of the body and blood of the risen Lord even though the appearances of bread and wine remain the same.[14] Lutherans and other Protestant denominations have generally preferred explanation of the Real Presence in terms of the doctrine of consubstantiation, namely, that there are now two substances present, the bread and the wine together with the Body and Blood of the risen Lord.[15] Finally, among some Roman Catholic and Protestant theologians in recent years, the notion of transignification has been proposed to explain the doctrine of the Real Presence, namely, that the symbolic meaning and value of the consecrated bread and wine are now such that they no longer serve as food and drink for ordinary consumption but only as a special form of sharing or interpersonal communion with the risen Lord.

What is important, however, is not the theoretical explanation of the doctrine of the Real Presence but its value as an expression of a felt need on the part of Christians for physical contact with their risen Lord and of a presumed need on the part of the Lord himself for sustained physical contact with his followers even after his departure from this life. A simple reading of the Last Supper narrative in the Synoptic Gospels makes clear the strong desire of Jesus to remain with his disciples even after his approaching death and to remain with them not simply as a fond memory but as a spiritual presence under the symbols of consecrated bread and wine (e.g., Luke 22:15: "I have eagerly desired to eat this Passover with you before I suffer"). Similarly, as the account of Jesus' appearance to the disciples on the way to Emmaus on Easter Sunday evening makes clear (Luke 24:13–35), the disciples were overjoyed by the unexpected physical presence of the risen Lord in their midst, even if only for a short time. Furthermore, the Eucharist obviously became the central ritual for the early Christians, not simply because it brought them together for mutual consolation and support, but because it provided them with regular physical contact with their risen Lord, albeit under the symbols of consecrated bread and wine.

There is then a physical or, in a sense, "erotic" dimension to God's love for us and our love for God. There is, in other words, a desire for physical or bodily contact with human beings on the part of God and with God on the part of human beings. Did the Son of God, for example, become incarnate simply to redeem us from our sins or in order to share human life with us here and now and thus to enable us eventually to share the life of the divine community in our risen bodies? Here I side with the great Franciscan medieval theologian Bonaventure rather than with Thomas Aquinas in the belief that the sharing of divine life rather than simply the redemption of sin was the deeper motive for the Incarnation.[16] Similarly, Paul expresses his longing to die and be with Christ physically in the new creation but recognizes the need to remain in this life a little longer for the sake of the brethren (Phil. 1:21–24). Finally, in the writings of various theologians, but above all in the writings of Christian mystics through the ages, we find a surprisingly physical or passionate love for the triune God and especially for the person of Jesus as the risen Lord.[17] Such passionate love of Christians for their risen Lord and of the Lord himself for physical contact with his followers is in my judgment the deeper significance of the traditional Christian belief in the doctrine of the abiding Real Presence of Jesus in the Eucharistic species.

Bernard Cooke links Eucharist and the sacrament of Matrimony along the same lines, given his prior understanding of Matrimony as a physical self-giving of a man and a woman to one another in a way that mirrors Christ's physical gift of self to the church through the Eucharist: "In their relationship to one another, and in proportion as that relationship in a given set of circumstances truly translates Christ's own self-giving, the couple are a sacrament to each other and a sacrament to those who know them."[18] As he further explains, for Jesus to give himself as food and drink to his followers is to combine into one physical action the two most central symbols of love and concern within the human family: "He took the giving of food, which is the most basic action of parents (beginning with a mother nursing her baby) [to] manifest their concern for their children, and he united its symbolism with that of the gift of the body in marital intercourse. Taking the bread, he said, 'This is my body given for you.'"[19]

Since marriage is fundamentally an erotic relationship between a man and a woman climaxing in periodic sexual intercourse, so Eucharist should also be seen as an erotic relationship between Christ and the Christian community. As part of the Eucharistic ritual, after all, first the community offers to Christ and the Father their corporate gift of self under the symbols of bread and wine, and then with the words of consecration the transformed symbols of bread and wine are offered to the community as a form of physical sharing or interpersonal communion with the risen Lord. Finally, keeping the consecrated hosts in a tabernacle or repository in a side chapel is a way of keeping the physical presence of the Lord in the church even after the Eucharistic ritual is completed. This practice began, to be sure, to assure the possibility of bringing Holy Communion to the sick or dying on short notice. But, as Roman Catholics over the centuries have implicitly testified by their actions, it also encourages the faithful to make periodic visits to the church in order to renew their desire for interpersonal exchange with the risen Lord.

Here the skeptic, of course, will object that it is an incredible stretch of the imagination to believe that Jesus even in his risen body is physically present in the Eucharist on altars and in tabernacles scattered throughout the world. In response, I refer the reader to an earlier chapter in this book ("In Whom We Live and Move and Have Our Being") in which I argued that we human beings and indeed all of material creation come forth from God, exist in God while in this life, and eventually return to God as the goal of our finite existence. Why then should it be such a problem to believe that Jesus is in the Eucharist when not only the consecrated bread and wine but all of God's creatures, ourselves included, are even now in God? Much depends, of course, on how we think of ourselves in God. Here I offer only a brief summary of what I already explained elsewhere.[20]

If the three divine persons by their ongoing interaction co-constitute an infinite or all-embracing field of activity, and if the world of creation as a vast network of interrelated fields of activity is located within that same all-encompassing divine field of activity, then Christ as the Incarnate Word of God can simultaneously exist in two fields of activity: the one proper to his divinity and the other proper to himself as a human being, Jesus of Nazareth. During his earthly life Jesus was free to reject the "Father's" initial aims and to distance himself from his own divinity. But after his death on the cross and resurrection, the link between his divinity and humanity became much stronger. In his risen life Jesus is physically present everywhere in creation where the Divine Word is present. Thus he is no longer subject to the limitations of space and time that we here and now experience. Yet, even though physically present everywhere in this world, he cannot be seen or touched by us directly.

This handicap or limitation, however, is overcome through Christ's gift of himself in the Eucharist. In this way Christ incorporates the consecrated bread and wine into his own divine-human field of activity and is present to us sensibly under these symbolic forms. Bread and wine, after all, are also Whiteheadian societies or structured fields of activity for their constituent actual occasions. If the humanity of Christ, body and soul, can be incorporated into the field of activity proper to the Divine Word, then through the words of consecration at the Eucharistic liturgy bread and wine can likewise be incorporated into the field of activity proper to Christ as the Incarnate Word. The bread and wine do not lose their physical reality as bread and wine through incorporation into the divine field of activity any more than the humanity of Jesus lost its physical reality when it was incorporated into the field of activity proper to the Divine Word. Somewhat akin to the Lutheran notion of consubstantiation, then, the consecrated bread and wine are still bread and wine, but they have taken on the new reality of being the Body and Blood of the risen Lord.[21] Though present everywhere in the universe through incorporation into the divine field of activity, Jesus as the risen Lord makes himself subject to the limitations of space and time through the consecrated bread and wine on altars and in tabernacles throughout the world. The consecrated bread and wine are his Eucharistic Body even as Christians gathered together in community throughout the world are Christ's mystical body. Christ is still very much present in our world, even though we can "see" him only with the eyes of faith.

Many years ago, in his book *The Risen Christ and the Eucharistic World*, Gustave Martelet developed further this same line of thought. As he saw it, the far deeper truth about the doctrine of the Real Presence is that not just bread and wine but all of creation, including the world of nature, are collectively becoming the Body of Christ.[22] All of created reality is being progressively integrated into the divine field of activity with the passage of time. With our fixation on the present moment and what is happening right now, we normally give little attention to the way that the past is steadily slipping away from us. It survives, to be sure, in our memories and even more importantly in the patterns of life that we inherit from the past. But it survives in a much fuller sense within the divine field of activity, the communitarian life that the three divine persons share with all their creatures. We proceed to an explanation of how this can happen in the next chapter.

CHAPTER 9

Alpha and Omega:
The Beginning and the End

Not only our individual life but also the universe is doomed to physical decay! This scientific insight of the twentieth century poses a great threat to theology and the faith of all religions. How can we believe in God and think of God and God's intentions with the world when human remembrance and history will finally come to an end? . . . [I]f the universe is finite, then there is only silence in the end. In the long run, everything will be in vain![1]

THESE SOBERING COMMENTS from the introduction to a set of essays on eschatology or the doctrine of "the last things" written by a group of scientists, philosophers, and theologians remind us of the challenge posed to classical Christian belief in eternal life by current work in the natural sciences. If our universe will someday come to an end in terms of either a "heat death" or a "deep freeze," then how can we continue to believe in the resurrection of the body and life everlasting? Are not our bodies likewise part of the material universe that is slowly coming to an end? How can scientists with religious convictions resolve the inevitable tension between the presuppositions of work in their discipline and their personal religious beliefs? Science seeks to explain events simply in terms of natural causes and effects within this world. Does this mean that as a matter of fact only this world exists and that appeal to

God and the world of the supernatural is an illusion which will sooner or later be set aside as a result of further progress in a scientific understanding of the world?

Certainly, if there is to be any worthwhile dialogue between philosophers and theologians, on the one hand, and scientists, on the other hand, both groups must be ready to take each other's truth claims seriously. Both are trying to say something important about the nature of reality and the place of human beings within it. Likewise, both groups should admit that they are working with imperfect models rather than strict blueprints in coming to terms with the world around them. Both, in other words, are working with symbolic representations of reality that resolve some questions and yet which leave many other questions still unanswered. The biggest question of all, of course, is whether these different models of reality can ultimately be seen as somehow complementary to one another rather than contradictory.

Is there, for example, any possibility of an intermediary position, an understanding of reality that would be compatible with the truth claims of both sides and thus provide a common language for the discussion of differing points of view? I believe that the metaphysics of intersubjectivity which I have set forth in these pages could serve this function. The philosopher on whom I mostly rely, Alfred North Whitehead, was a distinguished mathematician and physicist before becoming an equally renowned philosopher. As a result, he was able to critique his own work as a scientist in setting forth his philosophy. One of the key "mistakes" that he found in the science of his day was what he called the fallacy of simple location.[2] That is, scientists habitually presume that physical reality is ultimately made up of material atoms, tiny bits of matter with a specific location in space and time. All the things of this world are simply aggregates of these atoms, which in themselves never change. They simply exist in harmony with or in opposition to one another.

But, if atomism is in fact the case, then there is no evidence for the existence of spirit in our world. Spirit is by definition that which cannot be limited to simple location in space and time. We human beings, for example, are often deeply affected by people and organizations that are geographically far away but whose influence on us as family members, friends, or business associates is very strong. Through memory and imagination, we are, so to speak, both in the body and out of the body at the same time. We can be physically in one place and mentally somewhere else at the same time. Yet the tendency among natural scientists is to assume the opposite, at least when they are doing research in the laboratory. Human beings and all the other things of this world are strictly limited by the conditions of space and time; they can only be in one place at any given moment—exactly what Whitehead had in mind with his notion of the fallacy of simple location.

To overcome this mistaken assumption on the part of his fellow scientists, Whitehead proposed his own revolutionary hypothesis: namely, that the ultimate units of reality are not inert bits of matter with purely external relations to one another but rather momentary subjects of experience which have internal relations to all the other subjects of experience in their environment. Each momentary subject of experience is what it is only because it "prehends"—grasps on a feeling level—its specific relationship to other subjects of experience in its vicinity and then integrates all these feeling-level relationships into its own self-constitution here and now.[3] Physical reality, therefore, is not constituted by material atoms with purely accidental relations to one another but by momentary subjects of experience with necessary internal relations to one another. Nature is intrinsically interconnected and dynamic rather than simply spread out in space and time and basically lifeless.

Yet Whitehead himself in one respect remained an "atomist" because he did not think through carefully enough the way in which these momentary subjects of experience or actual occasions join together so as to form "societies" corresponding to the persons and things of commonsense experience. He imagined societies as groupings of actual occasions that are linked with one another by what he called a "common element of form" or analogous self-constitution.[4] Thus he failed to see that a society logically should be more than just an aggregate of constantly changing subjects of experience if it is to have some reality proper to itself. But then what is it? A society is not a still higher-level subject of experience or king-size actual occasion. Rather, as we have seen in previous chapters, it is a semipermanent field of activity or common space structured by the interplay of these same subjects of experience. In this way, it can give order and coherence to each new set of actual occasions and yet itself be subject to gradual modification in its structure with the passage of time.[5]

But what has all this to do with life after death and the possibility of the resurrection of the body? First of all, it suggests that spirit in some way or another is present at every level of existence and activity within Nature. The real things of which this world is made up are not material atoms with purely extrinsic relations to one another but momentary self-constituting subjects of experience in dynamic interrelation. The world is constituted by intersubjectivity even at the level of subatomic particles in their ever-changing patterns of relation to one another. Second, spirit never exists in total independence of material reality but always expresses or objectifies itself in some material way. Whitehead spoke of actual occasions as "subject/superjects." As subject an actual occasion is immaterial or purely spiritual, but as superject it is somehow material, something with a concrete shape or form for future actual occasions to prehend.[6] This is why I propose that actual occasions or subjects of experience by their interaction co-create a structured field of activity. The field is the outward expression or objective manifestation of their ongoing intersubjective relations. The field with its objective structure is what remains as individual subjects of experience come and go.[7]

Now, if we apply to the doctrine of the Trinity these remarks about momentary subjects of experience and the fields of activity that they co-constitute, then we can say that the three divine persons are likewise subjects of experience who by their ongoing relations with one another co-inhabit a structured field of activity or physical space for their life together. The field with its ongoing structure is the way in which they habitually objectify or express themselves to one another. In the language of classical Trinitarian theology, the structured field of activity is their divine nature or common ground of existence and activity.

Likewise, as I pointed out in chapter 1, we too live within this divine matrix or all-comprehensive field of activity proper to the divine persons. The world of creation is a vast network of interrelated and overlapping fields of activity for all the actual occasions at any moment within it, but the network itself is nested within the field of activity proper to the divine persons. Each of us by our decisions from moment to moment thus contributes first to the field of activity immediately around us, then to the world as a network of interrelated fields, but ultimately to the all-encompassing divine field of activity.

In this way, all the actual occasions or subjects of experience existing at any given moment (both divine and created) are linked together in co-creating a joint field of activity for their dynamic interrelation. This is what we mean by the kingdom of God as a reality that simultaneously exists both in heaven and on earth.

There is, then, a type of objective immortality being achieved at every moment within the process of creation, since what happens in the world immediately passes into the communitarian life of the three divine persons and becomes part, so to speak, of the history of God's dealings with the world. Yet, as we know from our personal experience, we have no awareness that we are thus being immortalized through incorporation into the divine life. Rather, limited by the conditions of existence in space and time, we and all other creatures in this world simply experience here and now an ongoing feeling of movement: either out of the future into the past or out of the past into the future. Only upon reflection does it occur to us that at every moment of our lives we are newly emergent from the divine matrix so as to exist for an instant as a subject of experience distinct from God but only so as to be immediately reincorporated into God—that is, into the divine matrix or divine field of activity. Thus what I am in virtue of the decision of the present moment will be forever preserved within the structured field of activity common to the three divine persons and all their creatures: the kingdom of God.

This still does not solve the problem of subjective immortality so that after death I actually experience myself as having come from God, having lived all my life unconsciously within God, and being now consciously reincorporated into God. To allow for this possibility, one must further say that at the moment of death each of us receives a special "initial aim" communicated to us by the power of God. In virtue of that initial aim we become conscious for the first time of being part of the divine matrix or divine field of activity. Thus consciously incorporated into God, we can take full possession of the field of activity that we have built up over the years through a lifetime of both conscious and unconscious decisions.

This will, of course, likewise be a moment of judgment for us as we finally come to terms with our own personal history and see how it fits into the all-encompassing divine matrix or divine field of activity. For some, this moment will undoubtedly be one of exhilaration because for the first time they realize the deeper meaning and value of their lives. They are not worthless but valuable in the eyes of God and their fellow human beings. For others, it may be more a moment of disappointment and chagrin when they realize how much they deceived themselves as to their own self-importance in the eyes of others. Finally, for perhaps most of us, it may be a blend of joy and sorrow, happiness and disappointment. In any case, the moment of judgment at the time of our death will be a moment of truth.

"Salvation" then depends upon whether we can thus accept the full truth about ourselves, albeit with the help of divine grace or God's forgiving love. The three divine persons, in other words, will be equivalently saying to each of us at the moment of our death: "We accept you and care for you as the person you have become over time. But do you accept and love yourself, given what you now know about yourself in the light of eternity? Can you accept the role which you de facto played in the history of the world around you, or do you need more time to think it over, so as to be reconciled to your failures as well as to rejoice in your successes in dealing with us and all your fellow creatures?"

This is, to be sure, only an imaginative reconstruction on my part of what happens at the moment of death, but it does make clear how the classical doctrine of the "four last things" can be still affirmed within this imaginative scheme—that is, if the "last things" are death, judgment, heaven, and hell, then all four are included. There are death and judgment, first of all, but not so much God's judgment on us as our own judgment on our past life. All the three divine persons do is to show us the full truth of our lives and ask us to accept it as a condition of full participation in the divine communitarian life. As Jesus in John's Gospel remarks, "The truth will set you free" (John 8:32). If one accepts the truth, then one is in "heaven," a state of full communion with the divine persons and the saints. If one refuses to accept the full truth about oneself, one is equivalently in "hell," a state of self-imposed alienation from the divine persons and the saints. One is still physically part of the divine communitarian life since nothing can exist outside of God. But presumably one is not enjoying ongoing life in God since one is inwardly tormented by one's own deeply felt hypocrisy in refusing to admit the truth about oneself. Finally, there is even room for "purgatory," if one for the moment vacillates between acceptance and refusal of God's offer of forgiveness on condition of accepting the truth about oneself. Within eternity there is ample opportunity to reflect on one's earthly life just ended.

But what about Christian belief in the resurrection of the body and the transformation of the physical universe at the end of the world? My argument is that the Last Judgment as depicted in the Bible is actually taking place at every moment of the cosmic process and human history. Since every actual occasion or momentary subject of experience comes into existence within God and is reincorporated into the divine life after its brief moment of self-constitution apart from God, then God's design for creation, the simultaneous vindication of both God's justice and God's mercy with respect to creatures, is being achieved at every moment, even if only for the moment. Naturally, we human beings are not aware of this ongoing divine judgment until the moment of our death, when we become fully aware of who we are and where we have been living all these years. But it is happening whether we realize it or not. As noted earlier, we live simultaneously in time and in eternity. Eternity is the togetherness of past, present, and future. So there is a glimpse of eternity in every "now" if only we take time to appreciate it.

In addition, if one accepts the logic of my argument, then certain obvious objections to the notion of eternal life from the viewpoint of natural science can be set aside. For example, a scientist may well ask which body one will possess in eternal life since the human body undergoes many transformations in the course of an ordinary lifetime. The bodies of an infant, a growing child, an adolescent, a young adult, a mature adult, a senior citizen, and a person at the point of death are all different from one another in size, strength, and quality of life. But if, as I have proposed, the human body is a complex structured field of activity for all the actual occasions existing within it at any given moment, then the body is far less physical and material than our senses here and now tell us. What is important about the body is the flow of energy from moment to moment in virtue of a fixed pattern of relations among the body parts. This pattern of relations can presumably be incorporated into the divine field of activity at every moment without difficulty and can be integrated with the pattern of relations governing our bodies from the first moment of conception onwards. When we die, therefore, we will be reunited with our bodies not as something that has passively suffered all the ravages of life in the body under various stresses but as the full and complete expression of our personalities, what we have over the years chosen to become in response to the many contingencies of life and what has thus been recorded in our characteristic bodily pattern of behavior. We will then easily recognize one another in eternity, but presumably at a higher level of perception than we enjoy in this life.[8]

Second, a scientist may object that human life will have become extinct long before the physical end of the universe, whether in terms of a "big crunch" or a "deep freeze." Hence, the biblical scenario for the coincidence of the Last Judgment and the end of the world is incompatible with the current state of research in physical cosmology.[9] Here I side with Kathryn Tanner in her belief that Christian eschatology has "no more stake in whether or how the world ends than a Christian account of creation has in whether or how the world had a beginning (say, by means of a big bang)."[10] Both the doctrine of creation and the classical understanding of Christian eschatology are vehicles for the expression of religious truth, the relation of human beings and the rest of creation to God, rather than for the articulation of scientific theory about the beginning and end of the universe.

The doctrine of Creation, after all, establishes the radical dependence of the world on God as its Creator, and this relation of dependence holds even if the world had no beginning and will never end.[11] For the same reason, argues Tanner, eschatology should not be oriented to the distant future, but to the "ongoing redemptive (rather than simply creative) relation to God that holds for the world of the past, present, and future."[12] This resonates well with my own belief that we are being assimilated into the divine life at every moment. The divine plan for the redemption of the human race and all of creation is thus silently being accomplished even though we creatures of space and time remain unaware of what is happening to us until the moment of death. In this way the end of the world can take place immediately for us when we die and for all other creatures as their time in this world comes to an end. For human beings in particular, judgment, final redemption, and peace will be available from the moment of death onwards in complete independence of the current state of the cosmic process.

Toward the end of his book *The God of Hope and the End of the World*, John Polkinghorne speculates whether nonhuman creation will share in the "new heaven and new earth" predicted in the book of Revelation (21:1–4). In his view, nonhuman species will surely survive but not individual members of the species: "Perhaps there will be lions in the world to come but not every lion that has ever lived."[13] But he makes an exception for domestic animals or pets "who could be thought to have acquired enhanced individual status through their interactions with humans. Perhaps they will have a particular role to play in the restored relationships of the world to come."[14] I disagree. If all entities of this world, even inanimate things, are societies of immaterial self-constituting subjects of experience in dynamic interrelation, then all of them should be incorporated into the divine communitarian life without exception, but inevitably they will be preserved within the divine life in different ways.

Animal species with a measure of self-awareness in this life should be able to take possession of the field of activity proper to their life history much like human beings. But they will not experience judgment, redemption, and peace in the same way as humans because they were not as responsible for their decisions while in this life. Lower-level animal species without self-awareness and all the various forms of plant life should still be able to experience a renewed sense of well-being within the divine life. Finally, not inanimate things as such but their dynamic components (atoms and molecules, even subatomic particles) should in principle be reenergized through participation in the divine life. They too are societies of actual occasions, immaterial subjects of experience that can be incorporated into the divine matrix or structured field of activity proper to the divine persons. Nothing, in other words, that comes into existence in virtue of divine initial aim and lives the divine life in conjunction with the three divine persons for however brief a time is ever completely destroyed. Everything is preserved, albeit in a transformed state.

My objection to Polkinghorne's thesis, therefore, is that in thinking about the transformation of the physical universe at the end of the world he still gives priority to spirit over matter as if they could be sharply separated from one another. Thus only human beings as created spirits par excellence and perhaps their household pets because of their privileged relation to human beings will survive as individuals in the world to come. All the other creatures of this world because of their materiality will only survive as token representatives of a material world that has ceased to be. But if, as I urged earlier, there is a necessary bond between matter and spirit such that neither can exist in total independence of the other, then everything physical or material in this world is spiritual in its own way and has some minimal right to exist in the world to come, even if not in the same way as it does here and now under the conditions of space and time.

Where Polkinghorne is precisely on target, however, is in his emphasis on relationality as the key to eternal life. Thus, not only pets in their relationship to their human owners, but all creatures will be incorporated into the divine matrix in terms of their relations to one another during this life. No thing, no plant, no animal, no human being can exist alone and for itself within the divine life. All become part of the divine communitarian life since it is the form of life proper to the three divine persons. The peculiar problem for us human beings, of course, is that alone among the creatures of this world we must consciously say yes to this total self-giving as the condition for participation in the divine life. Yet with the assistance of divine grace all things are possible. If we cooperate with the flow of divine life and love into our minds and hearts, it not only can happen but will happen.

CHAPTER 10

Science, Faith, and Altruism

VERY OFTEN in this book I have made reference to the collective power of good and evil and indicated that only when we rise above narrow self-interest do we genuinely contribute to the collective power of good in this world. Otherwise, without even thinking about it, when we become preoccupied either with our own personal interests or with the activities of the various groups to which we belong (church, local community, business corporations, etc.), we end up contributing to the unholy competition on which the collective power of evil thrives. In this chapter I want to take a critical look at this idea. Is it realistic to think that ordinary human beings (saints like Mother Teresa possibly excepted) can rise above narrow self-interest to genuine altruism, at least for any extended period of time? Is it contrary to human nature to put the interests of others on a par with, or even ahead of, our own needs and desires? Is constant self-giving love so rare that even with the assistance of divine grace it must remain an impossible dream rather than an achievable reality?

In recent years serious scientific research has been done on whether self-giving love or altruism is ultimately an illusion or an indispensable part of normal human existence. With assistance from the John Templeton Foundation, an Institute for

Research on Unlimited Love has been established at Case Western Reserve University in Cleveland, Ohio, under the direction of Dr. Stephen G. Post. Post and his staff bring together experts in various disciplines such as sociobiology, philosophy, psychology, and theology so as to investigate from a multidisciplinary perspective the phenomenon of self-giving love—how it arose in the course of human history and how it can be further cultivated in our own day.[1] Many scientists, of course, believe that this kind of research is ultimately a waste of time and money since human beings always act out of self-interest. In an evolutionary context where there is constant competition for survival, human beings have to act out of self-interest or risk extinction. Perhaps these scientists are right. To be fair, though, let us look at the arguments pro and con.

Theological reflection on the notion of self-giving love can be found already in the pages of the New Testament. One need only think of the Last Supper discourse of Jesus as recorded in John's Gospel (chs. 14-17), the First Letter of John (chs. 3-4), and the celebrated hymn to love in Paul's First Letter to the Corinthians (ch. 13). Likewise, philosophers like Charles Sanders Peirce and priest/scientists like Pierre Teilhard de Chardin have maintained that love is the dynamic principle at work in cosmic evolution.[2] But study of love simply as a human phenomenon by social scientists is of fairly recent origin. In 1945 the chairperson of the Department of Sociology at Harvard University, Pitirim Sorokin, founded the Harvard Research Center for Creative Altruism. Some years later in 1954 he published his major work on the science of altruism, *The Ways and Power of Love*.[3] In the preface to that book he asserts, "Only the power of unbounded love practiced in regard to *all human beings* can defeat the forces of interhuman strife, and can prevent the pending extermination of man by man on this planet."[4] Yet, as he notes, very little is known scientifically about love in comparison with other forms of physical energy like light, heat, and electricity.

Hence, he initially sets forth the ways in which love is at work in human life. The religious aspect of love is to be identified with God or Ultimate Reality; the ethical aspect with pure goodness; the ontological aspect with "creative energy or power" (thus much akin to the theories of Peirce and Teilhard de Chardin); the physical aspect with the interconnectedness of inanimate things; the biological aspect with the drive toward union and sexual reproduction among organisms; the psychological aspect with empathy, sympathy, kindness, devotion, respect, and so on; and finally, the social aspect of love with "meaningful interaction—or relationship—between two or more persons where the aspirations and aims of one person are shared and helped in their realization by other persons."[5]

To be able to measure degrees of love, Sorokin made use of still other categories: intensity, extensivity, duration, purity, and adequacy.[6] Intensity and extensivity of love, for example, tend to vary in inverse proportion; it is very difficult to love a wide range of people with the same degree of intensity. Similarly, high intensity in a love relationship tends to diminish with the passage of time, but the relationship might gain in other respects (e.g., purity and adequacy). Using these standards, Sorokin was able objectively to measure what was previously regarded as the arena of purely subjective feelings. Yet the results of his research were still held in suspicion by many other sociologists, if only because the scope of that research was interdisciplinary rather than sharply focused.[7]

Some years later another Harvard professor, Edward O. Wilson, advanced a more pragmatic explanation for altruistic behavior. He argued, "The biological principles which now appear to be working reasonably well for animals in general can be extended properly to the social sciences," that is, to sociology and the other disciplines dealing with human social behavior.[8] Genes, wherever they are found, operate in the same way according to the principle of natural selection. That is, they seek to reproduce themselves within the animal organism in which they are located.[9] Agreeing with Wilson, Richard Dawkins claims that "a predominant quality to be expected in a successful gene is ruthless selfishness."[10] Yet Dawkins also concedes that, if cooperation between members of a given species results in the long-term survival of the species in competition with still other species, then the genes that foster cooperation will survive better than genes that foster competition among the members of the species.

This is in some ways a bizarre approach to animal behavior, much less human behavior. That is, the genes seem to predetermine the way in which the organism as a whole operates rather than vice versa. Moreover, it seems to fly in the face of common human experience of genuinely altruistic behavior. Human beings are not always simply looking out for themselves so as to guarantee their own personal survival. They instinctively help one another in times of crisis even when this involves some risk for themselves. Wilson and Dawkins, however, have an explanation for this unselfish behavior on the part of human beings. "The answer is kinship: if the genes causing the altruism are shared by two organisms because of common descent, and if the altruistic act by one organism increases the joint contribution of these genes to the next generation, the propensity to altruism will spread through the gene pool."[11] That is, I am ready to help you in time of need even at some risk to myself because as members of the same family we share the same genes and have a mutual interest in seeing them perpetuated.

Wilson and Dawkins, of course, are not recommending selfish behavior on the part of human beings, but merely giving a biological explanation for our instinctive self-centered behavior. We spontaneously look out for members of the family in a time of crisis and only afterwards think of non-kin. If in fact we do help others outside our immediate family in time of crisis, on what basis do we do so, given that these other human beings do not share our gene pool? Wilson and Dawkins contend that a type of enlightened self-interest rather than pure altruism still prevails. In what is called "reciprocal altruism," one human being will spontaneously assist another human being outside of his kinship group in the implicit expectation that this other individual will someday reward the first individual or his kin group with similar acts of kindness or compassion.[12] In the end still self-interest rather than genuine unselfishness is still at work here.

Wilson and Dawkins have a good argument, yet common sense suggests that it is too simplistic. It ignores the broad impact of culture and tradition on our human behavior. Wilson himself concedes that human social evolution is "obviously more cultural than genetic."[13] But he still believes that natural selection, the urge of genes to propagate themselves in still other organisms, is ultimately responsible for human behavior. In that sense, "genes hold culture on a leash. The leash is very long, but inevitably values will be constrained in accordance with their effects on the gene pool. The brain is a product of evolution."[14] Yet, if Wilson is right, there is no higher purpose or meaning to human life or to the cosmic process as a whole. Everything is subordinated to the impersonal workings of natural selection in favoring some genes over others in the competition for survival and reproduction.

Are religion and appeals to the God-appointed order of things thus an illusion? Religions, says Wilson, play an important role in human life as "survival mechanisms": they assist us to cope better with the "ups and downs" of life in this world and thus give us an evolutionary advantage over those people who have no religious beliefs at all.[15] As Michael Ruse comments, what Wilson is doing here is turning science (in particular, his own discipline of sociobiology) into a secular religion.[16] Once human beings realize that religions, even with their appeal to self-transcendence in the service of a higher cause, are simply elaborate survival mechanisms in the evolutionary struggle, then they will surely turn to the results of scientific research on the human brain as the true basis for their ethical decisions. Science will thus always have the last word in competition for people's hearts and minds. Ruse himself is likewise a neo-Darwinian, someone committed to a strictly evolutionary approach to human behavior. While he too recognizes that religion plays an important role in the lives of most people,[17] he still thinks that there is no higher meaning or value to the evolutionary process. In the end, evolution "is a directionless process, going nowhere slowly."[18]

Fortunately, Stephen Pope, a philosopher/theologian at Boston College, provides a suitable compromise position between idealists and skeptics on this issue. Pope nicely combines insights from contemporary sociobiology with Thomas Aquinas's notion of the "order of charity" (*ordo caritatis*), the way in which love can and should be offered first to one's immediate family or kin and then in due measure to non-kin or even total strangers.[19] Pope points out, to be sure, that Aquinas's *ordo caritatis* has its own difficulties if only because the Aristotelian biology on which it is based is clearly out of date.[20] But, better than many contemporary Christians who have written about self-giving love, Aquinas realizes that there will inevitably be priorities in one's loving care for others. Likewise, Aquinas provides for those choices an objective basis that is grounded in the natural law rather than simply in subjective preference.

Both modern sociobiology and Thomistic ethical principles, therefore, make clear the naturalness of preferential love for family and close friends over concern for the needs of strangers. Likewise, both emphasize that human love is varied and flexible, taking different forms in different circumstances; yet the two disciplines likewise raise needed cautions for one another. Sociobiologists with their empirical research remind Thomists that legitimate love for self and kin can easily become disordered, leading to gross neglect of the more urgent needs of non-kin and total strangers. Thomists, with their appeal to natural law and the supernatural order, remind sociobiologists that biology alone does not provide adequate guidelines for human behavior. Only the biblical view of the human person as made in the image of God inspires a deep regard for human dignity that sharply contrasts with Dawkins's view of human beings as nothing more than "survival machines" for their genes.[21]

Yet here is where Pope's approach itself evidently needs more development. In outlining the links between Aquinas's *ordo caritatis* and contemporary sociobiology, Pope does not make sufficiently clear their differences. Aquinas grounds the *ordo caritatis* in natural law, which is the human understanding of the divine plan for the creation and eventual consummation of the cosmic process. It is as a result a thoroughly goal-oriented understanding of reality. The things of this world have divinely ordained "natures," which are ordered to one another within a world that is itself ordered from start to finish toward its Creator.[22] Contemporary sociobiology, on the contrary, makes no reference to a Creator God since neo-Darwinism is simply a synthesis of Darwin's principle of natural selection and the science of genetics. Consequently, as Michael Ruse noted above, evolution seems to be "a directionless process, going nowhere slowly."[23]

Stephen Pope has thus every reason to assert in opposition to sociobiologists like Wilson, Dawkins, and Ruse that there is a further explanation for altruistic behavior over and above kin preference and reciprocal altruism.[24] Belief in a Creator God who fashions human beings in the divine image and who assists them with divine grace to overcome the deeply rooted self-centered tendencies arising out of their evolutionary history profoundly alters how one looks at human nature. But still more is needed by way of explanation for human behavior.[25] What I have argued in this book is that all of reality, beginning with the three divine persons in their internal relations with one another, is based on mutual communication among dynamically interrelated subjects of experience. Altruism, self-giving love, is a necessary component in such an approach to reality. If all these interrelated subjects of experience do not somehow give themselves to one another, nothing happens. Everything collapses. The impulse toward union with others is not something optional for us human beings (and all other creatures) but a concrete imperative simply to survive and flourish in a necessarily interconnected world.

Here a contemporary feminist might respond to me in the words of Ronald Reagan debating with Jimmy Carter in the presidential campaign of 1980: "There you go again." Male philosophers and theologians have a way of extolling the idealism of self-giving love but then expect the women in their lives to be their servants while they themselves remain focused on their professional careers or even strictly personal desires.

In response I can only say that service of others must be voluntary, or it is a form of slavery. If women or men for whatever reason are trapped into involuntary servitude, they have a natural right to resist and to insist on being treated as equals in the sight of God and their contemporaries. But once their dignity as free human beings has been assured and they are able (at least in some measure) to choose without constraint their own path to self-fulfillment, then they too will face the same question as everyone else. Where do I most often find genuine self-fulfillment: in relentlessly pursuing my own interests no matter what the cost, or in sharing with others in projects that serve the common good but do not immediately offer me either a strong sense of personal achievement or the manifest gratitude of other people? Self-giving or self-sacrificing love will always remain for most of us an ideal to which we can never completely measure up. As the old saying has it, what we reach for is more important than what we actually grasp.

Still another obstacle to embracing fully this ideal of self-giving love might well be felt by men more than by women. Many men (and perhaps many women as well) find it more difficult to receive unselfish love from another than to offer it on their part to that other person. When they give of themselves spontaneously to another, they generally feel good because they have helped that other person and they instinctively judge that it was the right thing to do. But when they are the unexpected recipients of another's spontaneous care and concern, they often feel uneasy and wonder what they will have to do in return in order to compensate for what they have received.

What is unconsciously at work here, as I see it, is our deeply felt human desire to be independent and self-sufficient versus our belated recognition that this is impossible, that we cannot long survive without assistance from one another. Perhaps because of cultural conditioning, we men (more than women) tend to aim at self-sufficiency. In itself there is nothing wrong with wanting to be reasonably self-sufficient, not always in need of the help of other people simply to survive. But self-sufficiency is easily exaggerated so that one feels a deep sense of anxiety as soon as one realizes that one is no longer fully in control of one's own life and destiny. One has to trust in the basic goodwill of others to achieve one's goals, and this for men especially can be quite unsettling.

Yet here is where a scheme such as I have proposed in this book can have a healing and calming effect on both men and women. A metaphysics based on the notion of universal inter-subjectivity emphasizes interdependence rather than independence and self-sufficiency. Nothing of any consequence ever happens through individuals acting simply on their own and with regard only for their individual self-interest. Everything that lasts takes place in virtue of subjects of experience co-creating a shared field of activity and thereby setting up behavior patterns and intelligible structures that will have an impact on the future. Ironically, in the nonhuman world this is taken for granted. Sociobiologists tell us that with most animal species this happens instinctually, thus for the most part unconsciously, in the interests of survival and reproduction on the part of both individuals and groups. Edward O. Wilson was immensely impressed by the way in which ants, bees, and other social insects are seemingly hard-wired to sacrifice themselves for the survival and well-being of the larger group.[26] Likewise, among higher-order animals, the female instinctively protects her young against predators, even at risk to her own life.

Only we human beings regularly get it wrong in presuming that the supreme goal of life is to be independent and self-sufficient. As Jesus commented in Mark's Gospel (8:36–37), "What profit is there for one to gain the whole world and forfeit his life? What could one give in exchange for his life?" Something like a metaphysics of universal intersubjectivity is urgently needed to help contemporary human beings recognize what life in this world is really all about. Otherwise, as Pitirim Sorokin commented earlier, by our doggedly self-centered patterns of behavior both as individuals and as members of various social groups, we human beings may well face extinction as a species or at the very least end up doing considerable damage to the world in which we live.

Learning to Trust

IN THE *Dictionary of Biblical Theology* under the entry of "heart," we read:

> The connotations of the word *heart* are not the same in Hebrew and English. For us the heart is related to the affective life. From his heart, a man loves or hates, desires or fears. But the heart has no part in the intellectual life. The Hebrew uses *heart* to indicate a wider range of meaning, including all that is within a man. It stands for sentiments, but also memories, thoughts, reasoning, and planning. . . . The heart of man, therefore, is his whole conscious, intelligent, and free personality.[1]

Roman Catholics and other Christians who feel drawn to the person of Jesus under the symbol of the Sacred Heart clearly have in mind what the ancient Hebrews believed. They are looking for a fully interpersonal relationship with someone who is both divine and human, someone who is just as human as they are but who is likewise God Incarnate, one of the three divine persons. The image of the Sacred Heart conveys this strong sense of closeness between Jesus and ourselves. Yet the symbol of the heart is also a poignant reminder of the risks involved in interpersonal relationships. There are faithful hearts and there are cheating hearts. Can we trust ourselves to engage in a genuine heart-to-heart relationship with anyone, even with Jesus as God become human for our sake?

Scripture is full of references to the difficulty of a genuinely interpersonal relationship with God. In the first book of Samuel, for example, the Lord says to the prophet Samuel while Samuel is interviewing the sons of Jesse to see who should succeed Saul as king of Israel: "Not as man sees does God see, because man sees the appearance but the Lord looks into the heart" (1 Sam. 16:7). Likewise, the prophet Isaiah quotes the Lord as saying: "This people draws near with words only and honors me with their lips alone, though their hearts are far from me, and their reverence for me has become routine observance of the precepts of men" (Isa. 29:13). Hence, the first and greatest commandment of the Jewish Law has always been: "Hear, O Israel! The Lord is our God, the Lord alone! Therefore, you shall love the Lord your God, with all your heart, and with all your soul, and with all your strength. Take to heart these words which I enjoin on you today" (Deut. 6:4–6). If the heart is often the source of human rebellion against the Lord, it is also where reconciliation with the Lord must begin: "you shall seek the Lord, your God; and you shall indeed find him when you search after him with your whole heart and your whole soul" (Deut. 4:29).

Yet the prophets never cease reminding the people of Israel of their hardness of heart and the need for a change of heart, a new interior disposition toward Yahweh as their Lord and Savior. Speaking through Jeremiah, for example, God complains, "This people's heart is stubborn and rebellious; they turn and go away, and say not in their hearts: 'let us fear the Lord our God'" (Jer. 5:23-24). But God likewise promises a new covenant with the Jewish people: "This is the covenant which I will make with the house of Israel after those days, says the

Lord. I will place my law within them, and write it upon their hearts. I will be their God and they will be my people" (Jer. 31:33). In similar fashion, Ezekiel exhorts the people: "Cast away from you all the crimes you have committed, and make for yourselves a new heart and a new spirit" (Ezek. 18:31). But he later recognizes that this change of heart will come about through the action of God's grace more than through human resolve alone. Speaking in God's name, he says: "I will give you a new heart and place a new spirit within you, taking from your bodies your stony hearts and giving you natural hearts. I will put my spirit within you and make you live by my statutes, careful to observe my decrees" (Ezek. 36:26–27).

In the New Testament Jesus continues this tradition of referring to the heart as the symbol of the inner life of a human being and therefore as a potential source of both good and evil. In Matthew's Gospel, for example, while engaged in controversy with the Pharisees about ritual hand washing, Jesus exclaims: "For from the heart come evil thoughts, murder, adultery, unchastity, theft, false witness, blasphemy. These are what defile a person, but to eat with unwashed hands does not defile" (Matt. 15:19–20). At the same time, to the "clean of heart" he promises the vision of God (Matt. 5:8). He describes himself as "meek and humble of heart" (Matt. 11:29) and urges his disciples to follow his example, for "unless each of you forgives his brother from his heart" (Matt. 18:35), you will not receive forgiveness for your own sins from "God the Father." Finally, in the parable of the Sower of the Seed, he likens the human heart first to hardened ground in which the seed cannot take root and then to rich soil which produces an abundant harvest (Luke 8:11–15). So everything depends upon what is already happening in the interior life of a human being, that is, in his or her heart.

One finds frequent references to the heart in the Pauline epistles. In Romans 10:9–10, for example, one reads: "If you confess with your mouth that Jesus is Lord and believe in your heart that God raised him from the dead, you will be saved." The double reference to mouth and heart seems to indicate that Paul is aware of the gap that can sometimes exist between what one says and what one really believes. Again, in Ephesians 3:17–19, Paul prays "that Christ may dwell in your hearts through faith; that you, rooted and grounded in love, may have strength to comprehend with all the holy ones what is the breadth and length and height and depth, and to know the love of Christ that surpasses knowledge, so that you may be filled with all the fullness of God." First one must believe that Jesus is one's Lord and Savior and then, filled with gratitude, one will experience from the heart the overwhelming gift of God's love. Thus "the love of God has been poured into our hearts through the Holy Spirit that has been given to us" (Rom. 5:5). In the Spirit, Christians can appeal to God as "Father" (Gal. 4:6) and experience from the heart "the peace of God which surpasses all understanding" (Phil. 4:7).

Explicit references to the heart are less frequent in the Gospel according to John, but other metaphors are used to point to the subjectivity or interior life of the individual believer and the conversion of heart required of him or her so as to accept God's grace. To the Samaritan woman at the well, for example, Jesus promises "living water" that "will become in [her] a spring of water welling up to eternal life" (John 4:14), provided that she acknowledge him as the long-awaited Messiah. Likewise, in the farewell discourse after the Last Supper, Jesus prays that the Apostles and believers down through the centuries "may all be one, as you, Father, are in me and I in you, that they also may be one in us, that the world may believe that you sent me" (John 17:21). Only in this way "the love with which you loved me may be in them and I in them" (John 17:26). At the same time, Jesus cautions his disciples, "Let not your hearts be troubled or afraid" (John 14:27). There will inevitably be moments of insecurity and anxiety—above all, when Jesus himself is no longer physically present to them—but if they remain firm in their beliefs, their hearts will expand with Christ's peace, a peace that the world cannot give.

Perhaps the most explicit testimony to the way in which the human heart is sometimes conflicted is to be found in a celebrated passage out of the first letter of John:

> We have come to know and to believe in the love God has for us. God is love, and whoever remains in love remains in God and God in him. In this is love brought to perfection among us, that we have confidence on the day of judgment because as he is, so are we in this world. There is no fear in love, but perfect love drives out fear because fear has to do with punishment, and so one who fears is not yet perfect in love. We love because he first loved us. (1 John 4:16–19)

The author initially professes his belief in God's love for him. Yet he also recognizes the challenge that the expectation of future divine judgment poses to that same belief. In the end, he reaffirms his belief in God's love for him but tacitly seems to acknowledge that his love is not yet perfect because fear is still somehow a part of his relationship with God. Perfect love still remains something to strive for.

Here we may pause to ask why these conflicted feelings arose in the mind and heart of the sacred author and why we too have perhaps felt the same ambiguity in our relationship with God. Is it simply a nagging awareness of our own sinfulness that troubles us or is it perhaps something deeper yet in our psyche of which we are not fully aware? As I see it, the deeper reason for this insecurity lies in the very nature of the intersubjective relationship that we seek to establish with God. We are not fully in touch with our own subjectivity; hence, we cannot guarantee to ourselves that we will never abandon our relationship to God. But we also are not able to fathom the divine subjectivity so as to know with absolute certainty how God will deal with us in the future. So it is in every human intersubjective relationship where two people only very gradually come to trust one another deeply. So it must also be in our relationship with God. Perfect love drives out fear, but perfect love of God remains something to be striven for rather than something already achieved.

To illustrate my point, I refer here to passages out of both the Hebrew Bible and the New Testament where the sacred writer expresses a holy fear before the mystery of the divine subjectivity. Adam and Eve, for example, were afraid of God after they sinned because they were not sure how God would respond to their infidelity (Gen. 3:8). They lost the innocence of children playing in a garden of delights because for the first time they became aware of their own willfulness and feared the consequences of divine judgment. Similarly, Noah and his family had to be reassured of God's continuing fidelity to them through the appearance of a rainbow in the sky after the flood waters abated (Gen. 9:12–16). Finally, Moses encounters God in the burning bush but is told to keep his distance and remove the sandals from his feet, "for the place where you stand is holy ground" (Exod. 3:5). The sacred writer then adds, "Moses hid his face, for he was afraid to look at God," afraid of a direct interpersonal relationship with God (Exod. 3:6). On another occasion, of course, Moses wanted to see God face to face, but God replies, "My face you cannot see, for no man sees me and still lives" (Exod. 33:20). Hence, Moses is permitted a view of God only from the rear.

Among the prophets of Israel, there is regular reference to the wrath of God, sometimes directed toward the people of Israel and other times directed toward their enemies, but in both cases revealing the divine subjectivity, God's evident displeasure with what is currently happening within creation. Isaiah, for example, describes the wrath of God against Assyria as follows: "His lips are filled with fury, his tongue like a consuming fire" (Isa. 30:27). But God's fury is also exercised against the people of Israel: "I myself will fight against you with outstretched hand and mighty arm, in anger, and wrath, and great rage!" (Jer. 21:5-7). Yet God's wrath toward the Israelites is always tempered by God's mercy: "In an outburst of wrath, for a moment I hid my face from you. But with enduring love I take pity on you, says the Lord, your redeemer" (Isa. 54:8). Likewise, in a celebrated passage from Hosea, God says, "I will not destroy Ephraim again. For I am God, not man, the Holy One present among you" (Hos. 11:8-9). What stands out in all these passages is the divine subjectivity. God is personally, even passionately, involved with God's people.

Still another glimpse into the divine subjectivity is provided by the way in which Job eventually comes to terms with the mystery of divine providence in his life. As we have seen in earlier chapters of this book, we cannot always fathom how God is ordering what happens in this world in terms of a larger scheme of things. Initially, Job accepts with admirable equanimity his multiple misfortunes. But goaded by the charge that he must somehow be responsible for whatever has happened to him, he defends his innocence with passion and lodges a complaint against God. At this point the Lord speaks to Job "out of the storm" and addresses to him a series of questions:

Where were you when I founded the earth? Tell me, if you have understanding. Who determined its size; do you know? Who stretched out the measuring line for it? . . . And who shut within doors the sea, when it burst forth from the womb; when I made the clouds its garment and thick darkness its swaddling bands? . . . Which is the way to the dwelling place of light, and where is the abode of darkness, that you may take them to their boundaries and set them on their homeward paths? (Job 38:4–20)

Job acknowledges his arrogance in protesting against the mysterious ways of divine providence: "I have dealt with great things that I do not understand; things too wonderful for me, which I cannot know. . . . Therefore I disown what I have said, and repent in dust and ashes" (Job 42:3, 6). In effect, Job has come in contact with the mystery of the divine subjectivity and is humbled: "I had heard of you by word of mouth, but now my eye has seen you" (Job 42:5). Job is saying, "I feel your mysterious presence and activity in my life," and at least for now, that is enough.

Turning now to the New Testament, we note, first of all, that Jesus clearly had a warm filial relationship with his "Father" in heaven. When asked by his disciples how to pray, he urges them to address God as a loving Father caring for his children (Matt. 6:9–15; Luke 11:2–4). But Jesus also experienced tension and stress in his relationship with the Father at key moments in his life. During his agony in the garden on the night before he died, for example, he prayed, "Father, if you are willing, take this cup away from me; still not my will but yours be done" (Luke 22:42). Even more poignantly, while dying on the cross, he felt alone and forsaken by the God to whom he had been so devoted: "My God, my God, why have you forsaken me?"

(Mark 15:34). Hence, at least in his human consciousness, Jesus experienced desolation periodically in his efforts to maintain loving contact with God as his Father. Like Job, he too had to put his trust blindly in God's care for him even when evidence of that loving concern was notably lacking.

In a celebrated passage out of the Epistle to the Romans, Paul also seems to reflect the difficulty of remaining faithful to God while under persecution:

> What will separate us from the love of Christ? Will anguish, or distress, or persecution, or famine, or nakedness, or peril, or the sword? As it is written: "For your sake we are being slain all the day; we are looked upon as sheep to be slaughtered." No, in all these things we conquer overwhelmingly through him who loved us. For I am convinced that neither death, nor life, nor angels, nor principalities, nor present things, nor future things, nor powers, nor height, nor depth, nor any other creature will be able to separate us from the love of God in Christ Jesus our Lord. (Rom. 8:35-39)

The impassioned rhetoric of this passage would argue that Paul too at intervals experienced discouragement and even desolation in his relationship with God but refused to give up his heartfelt conviction that in the person of Jesus God had revealed a deep and abiding love for all human beings.

Even with respect to his Jewish brothers and sisters who had thus far refused to acknowledge Jesus as the Messiah, Paul was confident that God's love for them would eventually prevail. "For the gifts and call of God are irrevocable" (Rom. 11:29). In the meantime, of course, patience is required. "For who has known the mind of the Lord and who has been his counselor? Or who has given him anything that he may be repaid?" (Rom. 11:34-35). Once again the mystery of the divine subjectivity in dealing with human beings becomes clear. All that Paul, like Job before him, can do is humbly to acknowledge his human limitations and to put his trust in God's loving care both for himself and all other creatures: "Oh, the depths of the riches and wisdom and knowledge of God! How inscrutable are his judgments and how unsearchable his ways" (Rom. 11:33).

Mystery is then inevitably associated with God's relationship to us and our relationship to God. Part of the mystery lies in our own inability to fathom the depths of our own subjectivity. Paul alludes to this problem when he says, "Among human beings, who knows what pertains to a person except the spirit of the person that is within?" (1 Cor. 2:11). But how many of us are truly in touch with our own inner spirit, still less with the divine "Spirit" who "scrutinizes everything, even the depths of God" (1 Cor. 2:10)? Hence, if we have trouble understanding our own ever-changing feelings and desires, how are we to comprehend the mind and heart of God? Yet Paul is confident that this is indeed possible since "we have the mind of Christ" (1 Cor. 2:16). That is, as the hymns at the beginning of the Epistle to the Ephesians and again at the beginning of the Epistle to the Colossians abundantly make clear, we have in the life and teachings of Jesus—but above all in his passion, death, and resurrection—the key to understanding the mind of God with respect to ourselves:

> Blessed be the God and Father of our Lord Jesus Christ, who has blessed us in Christ with every spiritual blessing in the heavens, as he chose us in him, before the foundation of the world, to be holy and without blemish before him. In love he destined us for adoption to himself through Jesus Christ, in accord with the favor of his will, for the praise of the glory of his grace that he granted us in the beloved. (Eph. 1:3–6)

There is no overt reference here to the heart of Christ and therewith to the heart or subjectivity of God the Father. But insofar as we put our faith in the divine plan for the salvation of the world, that which was chosen by God the Father before the foundation of the world and only now made manifest in the person of Christ, the mind and heart of God are revealed to us. In and through the power of the Holy Spirit, the Christian can accept in full confidence what an unbeliever might well regard as wishful thinking or romantic nonsense.

The mystery of intersubjectivity, therefore, is never eliminated even after one has come to accept Jesus Christ as one's personal Lord and Savior. Much the same as in normal human relations, one must continue to grow in a trusting relationship to God the Father in and through a personal relationship to his "Son," Jesus Christ, all in the power of the Holy Spirit. The symbol of the heart of Christ, as revealed to Saint Margaret Mary Alacoque and as propagated ever since in terms of devotion to the Sacred Heart of Jesus, is thus a convenient focal point for an intersubjective relationship with God, which is implicitly offered to us on every page of the Hebrew Bible and the New Testament. The symbol of the heart, to be sure, always remains ambiguous. As a representation of the subjectivity or inner life of the individual human being, it is simultaneously a reminder of human infidelity (a "cheating heart") and an invitation to intimacy that is almost irresistible. But in the context of our relationship to God, the symbol of the heart is a clear and unmistakable reminder of God's fidelity to us and persevering love for us. As John Stackhouse comments, "If Jesus is the human face of God, . . . then we can trust God in spite of the evil all around us and in us."[2] We are capable of an enduring relationship with the three divine persons because they have first loved us and continue to support us in our efforts at union first

fellow creatures but ultimately with themselves
: never-ending kingdom of God. Not the collective
power of evil, but rather the collective power of good in the
end will prevail.

I conclude this chapter and this book with a backward look
at what I have proposed here and a short personal reflection. In
the introduction I suggested that we should think of ourselves
as coming forth from God (understood as the "divine matrix"
or ground of our being) and return to God as members of a cosmic community, participating with the divine persons in their
own communitarian life. As I mentioned in chapter 1, this is
only a model or symbolic representation of something that
our minds cannot comprehend, the God-world relationship in
all its fullness. But models are important for us to feel at home
in our world and at peace with ourselves, the world around us
and the God we worship. Without some comprehensive vision
of what life is all about, we feel all too often confused and dis-
couraged in the face of the inevitable ups and downs of every-
day life.

The image of ourselves as coming forth from God as pure
gift—living in the presence of the divine persons all our lives
(whether consciously or not), and at the end of our lives return-
ing to God to share with all our fellow creatures in the riches
of the divine life, the ongoing drama of creation and redemption on a cosmic scale—is very encouraging and consoling,
above all in life's difficult moments. Naturally, this is not a
blueprint of the way things really are, but it still encourages us
to live with a little more daring and verve, more creatively as I
suggested in chapter 2: to rely on the divine initial aims coming our way at every moment and to trust that things will work
out if we do our best to remain faithful to divine guidance.
Indeed, we can hope that they will not just work out for our-

selves as individuals here and now but will have consequences for others extending far into the future. As I mentioned in chapter 8, the divine persons are taking care of the bigger picture for us. In the end, it is simply a matter of learning to trust that all will be well.

Now for the concluding personal reflection. As a young man I became a novice or candidate for membership in the Society of Jesus, a community of men religious within the Roman Catholic Church. In my first year of candidacy I made the *Spiritual Exercises* of Saint Ignatius of Loyola, the founder of the Jesuits, and found them quite challenging and difficult to accept. While the opening meditation, the "Principle and Foundation," appealed to my sense of what was reasonable, subsequent meditations on the life of Christ threw me into confusion and self-doubt about my vocation. The "Principle and Foundation," after all, simply urged me to be prudent in using the good things of this world so as not to jeopardize the ultimate goal of human life, which is "to praise, reverence, and serve God our Lord," and by this means to save one's soul.[3] But subsequent meditations in the course of the *Exercises* focused on the image of Christ on the cross dying for my sins and urged me to reflect, "What have I done for Christ? What am I doing for Christ? What ought I to do for Christ?"[4] Still later I was asked to respond wholeheartedly to the call of Christ to follow him in his selfless efforts to bring about the kingdom of God on earth, even if it meant embracing with Christ actual poverty and mistreatment by other human beings.[5] Finally, in the concluding meditation of the *Exercises*, the "Contemplation to Attain Love," I was reminded of all God's gifts to me, God's presence and activity in my life, and urged to make an act of complete self-surrender to the divine will, asking only for the grace to love God in some fashion as God has always loved me.[6]

These meditations upset me since I was not at all sure that I was capable of such generosity. But with gentle counseling from the Jesuit novice master, I persevered as a novice and took my "First Vows." Some fifty-six years later I am still a Jesuit and, while still a bit uneasy with the ideal of complete self-surrender to the divine will, belatedly have to come to realize the wisdom of the strategy of Ignatius in the *Spiritual Exercises*. Appeals to reason and enlightened self-interest will never move me or anyone else to real generosity in the service of God and our neighbor, at least on a regular basis. Only the experience of being loved by God and responding to God's love inspires that measure of self-giving. In the end, then, divine grace, not human resolve, proves victorious. In our human weakness we beg for the gift of God's love and try to remain faithful to the unmistakable signs of that love both in the person of Christ and in the behavior of those who care for us and whom we too try to love.

Notes

Introduction

1. See, e.g., Elizabeth A. Johnson, *She Who Is: The Mystery of God in Feminist Theological Discourse* (New York: Crossroad, 1992); Rosemary Radford Ruether, *Sexism and God-Talk: Toward a Feminist Theology* (Boston: Beacon, 1983); Elizabeth Schüssler Fiorenza, *In Memory of Her: A Feminist Theological Reconstruction of Christian Origins* (New York: Crossroad, 1983); Sandra M. Schneiders, *Women and the Word: The Gender of God in the New Testament and the Spirituality of Women* (New York: Paulist, 1986); and many others.

Chapter 1

1. Thomas Aquinas, *Summa Theologiae* (Madrid: Biblioteca de Autores Cristianos, 1951), 1, q.8, a.1.
2. Ibid., a.2.
3. Ibid., a.3.
4. Sallie McFague, *Models of God: Theology for an Ecological, Nuclear Age* (Philadelphia: Fortress Press, 1987).
5. Ibid., 63.
6. Ian G. Barbour, *Religion and Science: Historical and Contemporary Issues*, rev. ed. (San Francisco: HarperSanFrancisco, 1997), 119.
7. McFague, *Models of God*, 73.
8. Ibid., 75.
9. Ibid., 72. See also Charles Hartshorne, *Man's Vision of God and the Logic of Theism* (Hamden, CT: Archon Books, 1964), 230–32.
10. McFague, *Models of God*, 76.
11. Ibid., 77.
12. Ibid., 78.
13. Alfred North Whitehead, *Process and Reality: An Essay in Cosmology*, corrected ed., ed. David Ray Griffin and Donald W. Sherburne (New York: Free Press, 1978), 18.

14. McFague also thinks of God in threefold terms, namely, as Mother, Lover, and Friend to her creatures (*Models of God*, 78–87). But this is really not a Trinity composed of three distinct divine persons but only the three functions or "faces" of God to the world.

15. See Martin Buber, *I and Thou*, trans. Roland Gregor Smith (New York: Scribner's, 1970), 37–72.

CHAPTER 2

1. Alfred North Whitehead, *Process and Reality: An Essay in Cosmology*, corrected ed., ed. David Ray Griffin and Donald W. Sherburne (New York: Free Press, 1978), 21.

2. Ibid., 31.

3. Ibid., 88.

4. Ibid., 18.

5. Ibid., 34.

6. Ibid., 88.

7. Alfred North Whitehead, *Science and the Modern World* (New York: Free Press, 1967), 179.

8. Whitehead, *Process and Reality*, 21. Whitehead, to be sure, had in mind here the way in which an actual occasion gathers together diverse features out of its own past and the past of the world to which it belongs and integrates them into the dynamic unity of its own self-constitution here and now. I am using that same notion of the many becoming one in another context, not foreseen by Whitehead, as will be evident below.

9. Ibid., 244.

10. Ibid., 189.

11. See below, chap. 7.

12. Whitehead, *Process and Reality*, 88.

13. Thomas Aquinas, *Summa Theologiae* (Madrid: Biblioteca de Autores Cristianos, 1951), I, Q. 3, a. 4.

14. See below, chap. 7.

15. There are, to be sure, two schools of thought among scientists on the subject of indeterminacy in Nature, above all at the subatomic level of investigation. One group would argue that the indeterminacy is simply due to the limitations of our current technology and that in time with improved research instruments a seamless web of natural causes and effects will explain all events at the subatomic level and elsewhere in Nature. The other group would argue that indeterminacy is an objective feature of Nature and not a limitation of current human knowledge (see on this point Ian G. Barbour, *Religion and Science: Historical*

and Contemporary Issues [San Francisco: HarperCollins, 1997], 170–73). The neo-Whiteheadian scheme that I have presented in this chapter is in agreement with the second school of thought. If, as Whitehead claims, "the final real things of which the world is made up" are actual occasions or momentary self-constituting subjects of experience, then indeterminacy is, as noted above, an objective feature of Nature at all levels of existence and activity.

CHAPTER 3

1. Norman Pittinger, *Cosmic Love and Human Wrong* (New York: Paulist, 1978), 46.
2. Many scientists would distinguish sharply between spontaneity within physical organisms and indeterminacy at the subatomic level of existence and activity and attribute the latter at least sometimes to imprecision in human systems of measurement and analysis (see here Ian G. Barbour, *Religion and Science: Historical and Contemporary Issues* [San Francisco: HarperCollins, 1997], 170–73). But within a Whiteheadian scheme of things, one can attribute a measure of spontaneity to actual occasions even at the subatomic level since all actual occasions are by definition self-constituting subjects of experience.
3. Holmes Rolston III, "Naturalizing and Systematizing Evil," in *Is Nature Ever Evil? Religion, Science and Value*, ed. Willem B. Drees (London: Routledge, 2003), 67–86.
4. Karl Rahner, *Foundations of Christian Faith: An Introduction to the Idea of Christianity*, trans. William V. Dych (New York: Crossroad, 1978), 226.
5. Peter Hodgson, *New Birth of Freedom* (Philadelphia: Fortress, 1976), 216–17.
6. Lisa Sergio, *Jesus and Woman* (McLean, VA: EPM Publications, 1975), 1–9.
7. Ibid., 53.
8. See here Wolfhart Pannenberg, *Systematic Theology*, vol. 1, trans. Geoffrey Bromiley (Grand Rapids: Eerdmans), 310: "Precisely by distinguishing himself from the Father, by subjecting himself to his will as his creature, by thus giving place to the Father's claim to deity as he asked others to do in his proclamation of the divine lordship, [Jesus] showed himself to be the Son of God and one with the Father who sent him (John 10:30)." Pannenberg is insistent that the obedience of the Son to the Father is paradoxically the basis for the independence of the Son from the Father within the divine life. In similar fashion Jesus in his human nature and all other creatures (but especially human beings) are simultaneously both one with the Father and separate from the Father

in their joint submission to the Father's will for the ongoing co-creation of the kingdom of God.

9. Arthur C. McGill, *Suffering: A Test of Theological Method* (Philadelphia: Westminster, 1982), 76.

10. Sigmund Freud seems to come to much the same conclusion on purely secular grounds in *Civilization and Its Discontents*, trans. James Strachey (New York: W. W. Norton, 1961), 69, where he links single-minded pursuit of the pleasure principle with Thanatos, the death instinct, and the impulse to form community with others as the expression of Eros, the life instinct. As he comments, "This struggle is what all life essentially consists of, and the evolution of civilization may therefore be simply described as the struggle for life of the human species."

CHAPTER 4

1. Reinhold Niebuhr, *The Nature and Destiny of Man*, 2 vols. (New York: Scribner's, 1964), 1:208.

2. See Langdon Gilkey, *Reaping the Whirlwind* (New York: Crossroad, 1976), 26.

3. Arthur C. McGill, *Suffering: A Test of Theological Method* (Philadelphia: Westminster, 1982), esp. 34–52.

4. Ibid., 50.

5. Pierre Teilhard de Chardin, *The Phenomenon of Man*, trans. Bernard Wall (New York: Harper & Row, 1959), 203–15.

6. Most scholars familiar with Matthew's Gospel agree that the author reedited the traditions present in Mark and other early sources so as to deal among other issues with a developing ecclesiology within his own community. See, e.g., William Thompson, S. J., *Matthew's Advice to a Divided Community*, Analecta Biblica 44 (Rome: Biblical Institute Press, 1970); also Jack Dean Kingsbury, "The Figure of Peter in Matthew's Gospel as a Theological Problem," *Journal of Biblical Literature* 98 (1979): 67–83, esp. 76–80.

7. See here Thomas Parker, "The Political Meaning of the Doctrine of the Trinity: Some Theses," *Journal of Religion* 60 (1980): 165–84, where he argues that the early Christian church, after a brief period of experimentation with various forms of charismatic leadership, became strongly monarchical in its internal government and quite judgmental in its attitude toward non-Christians. The ideal of the kingdom of God, therefore, as the human counterpart of the trinitarian community of divine persons and thus as a community of all men and women on an equal footing, was apparently subordinated to the felt needs of the

institutional church to survive in a world of competing ideologies and religious sects.

CHAPTER 5

1. Bernard Lee, S.M., *The Becoming of the Church: A Process Theology of the Structure of Christian Experience* (New York: Paulist, 1974), 172–78.
2. Ibid., 178–79.
3. Ibid., 182–83.
4. Tu Wei-Ming, "Confucianism," in *Our Religions*, ed. Arvind Sharma (San Francisco: HarperCollins, 1993), 143.
5. Ibid., 145.
6. Huston Smith, *The World's Religions: Our Great Wisdom Traditions* (San Francisco: HarperCollins, 1991).
7. Joseph A. Bracken, S.J., *The Divine Matrix: Creativity as Link between East and West* (Maryknoll, NY: Orbis, 1995).

CHAPTER 6

1. Bernard Lonergan, *Method in Theology* (New York: Herder & Herder, 1972), 292.
2. Josiah Royce, *The Problem of Christianity*, 2nd ed. (Chicago: University of Chicago Press, 1969), 340–41: "In the concrete, then, the universe is a community of interpretation whose life comprises and unifies all the social varieties and all the social communities which, for any reason, we know to be real in the empirical world which our social and historical sciences study. The history of the universe, the whole order of time, is the history and the order and the expression of this Universal Community."
3. Ibid., 273–95.
4. Ibid., 312–19.
5. Ibid., 387–88.
6. Ibid., 318.
7. Alfred North Whitehead, *Process and Reality: An Essay in Cosmology*, corrected ed., ed. David Ray Griffin and Donald W. Sherburne (New York: Free Press, 1978), 18.
8. Ibid., 27–28.
9. See above, n. 2.

CHAPTER 7

1. Augustine, *Confessions*, 11.14, in *Basic Writings of Saint Augustine*, ed. Whitney J. Oates (New York: Random House, 1948), 1:191.
2. Ibid.
3. Lawrence W. Fagg, *The Becoming of Time: Integrating Physical and Religious Time* (Atlanta: Scholars Press, 1995), 16–18.
4. Alfred North Whitehead, *Process and Reality: An Essay in Cosmology*, corrected ed., ed. David Ray Griffin and Donald W. Sherburne (New York: Free Press, 1978), 347.
5. Plato, *Timaeus*, nn. 37–38, in *The Dialogues of Plato*, 2 vols., trans. B. Jowett (New York: Random House, 1937), 2:19.
6. Robert Cummings Neville, *Eternity and Time's Flow* (Albany: State University of New York Press, 1993).
7. Ibid., 111.
8. See Plato, *Timaeus*, nn. 37–38, where the Demiurge or Creator is described as "immovably the same" and thus as always existing in the present, without past or future. Plato's concept of the timelessness of the deity was uncritically accepted by Augustine and the medieval tradition (including Thomas Aquinas) as likewise appropriate to the Trinity, even though according to Christian belief God is personally involved in creation through the Divine Word and the Holy Spirit.
9. Thomas Aquinas, *Summa Theologiae* (Madrid: Biblioteca de Autores Cristianos, 1951), 1, q.14, a.13, resp.
10. Ibid., q.45, a.2, resp.
11. Harold S. Kushner, *When Bad Things Happen to Good People* (New York: Schocken Books, 1989), 113–31, esp. 127: "The God I believe in does not send us the problem; He gives us the strength to cope with the problem."
12. See *The Spiritual Exercises of Saint Ignatius*, trans. George E. Ganss, S.J. (Chicago: Loyola University Press, 1992), 121–28, 189–95.

CHAPTER 8

1. Harold S. Kushner, *When Bad Things Happen to Good People* (New York: Schocken Books, 1989), 113–14.
2. Ibid., 125.
3. Ibid., 121.
4. Bernard Cooke, *Sacraments and Sacramentality* (Mystic, CT: Twenty-Third Publ., 1983).
5. Ibid., 2.
6. Ibid., 31.

7. Ibid., 112.

8. Ibid., 115–16.

9. Ibid., 116.

10. Ibid., 121.

11. Ibid., 123.

12. Ibid., 151.

13. Ibid., 155.

14. See *Enchiridion Symbolorum: Definitionum et Declarationum de Rebus Fidei et Morum*, ed. Henricus Denzinger and Adolphus Schönmetzer, S.J., 33rd ed. (Freiburg in Breisgau: Herder, 1965), n. 1642.

15. See *The Book of Concord: The Confessions of the Evangelical Lutheran Church*, trans. Theodore G. Tappert in collaboration with Jaroslav Pelikan, Robert H. Fischer, and Arthur C. Piepkorn (Philadelphia: Fortress, 1959), 575–76.

16. See Denis Edwards, *The God of Evolution: A Trinitarian Theology* (New York: Paulist, 1999), 31–32.

17. See Bernard McGinn, "God as Eros: Metaphysical Foundations of Christian Mysticism," in *New Perspectives on Historical Theology*, ed. Bradley Nassif (Grand Rapids: Eerdmans, 1996), 189–209. See also a new book (in process) by my colleague at Xavier University, Gillian Ahlgren, who has made a detailed study of the theme of erotic love in the writings of women mystics, including Julian of Norwich and Teresa of Avila.

18. Cooke, *Sacraments and Sacramentality*, 91.

19. Ibid., 95.

20. See also Joseph A. Bracken, S.J., "The Body of Christ—An Intersubjective Interpretation," *Horizons* 31 (2004): 7–21.

21. Transubstantiation was developed as a theory to explain the presence of Jesus in the Eucharist only because in terms of classical metaphysics one substance cannot assimilate, or otherwise take over the functions of, another substance without destroying the ontological integrity of the latter, i.e., without reducing the other substance to an accidental modification of itself as in the ingestion of food and drink. Hence, there had to be a miraculous change of substances in order that Jesus could be truly present in the consecrated bread and wine. The Lutheran doctrine of consubstantiation, however, is likewise defective since it gives no philosophical explanation of how two substances can coexist within the same physical reality such as I have presented in this chapter and elsewhere.

22. Gustave Martelet, *The Risen Christ and the Eucharistic World*, trans. Rene Hague (New York: Seabury, 1976), 160–79.

CHAPTER 9

1. John Polkinghorne and Michael Welker, eds., *The End of the World and the Ends of God: Science and Theology on Eschatology* (Harrisburg, PA: Trinity Press International, 2000), 1.

2. Alfred North Whitehead, *Science and the Modern World* (New York: The Free Press, 1967), 58.

3. Alfred North Whitehead, *Process and Reality: An Essay in Cosmology*, corrected ed., ed. David Ray Griffin and Donald W. Sherburne (New York: Free Press, 1978), 41–42.

4. Ibid., 34.

5. See Whitehead, *Adventures of Ideas* (New York: The Free Press, 1967), 204, where he notes the similarity between his own notion of society and the concept of substance in classical metaphysics, but then fails to develop the issue any further.

6. Whitehead, *Process and Reality*, 27–28.

7. See ibid., 87, where Whitehead refers to the "objectifications" of actual entities which "constitute the efficient causes" out of which a subsequent actual entity arises. But he seems not to have realized that an actual occasion precisely as "objectified" is a material as well as a purely spiritual reality.

8. Given this explanation of the resurrection of the body, how is one to interpret the bodily appearances of Jesus after his resurrection to Mary Magdalene and the apostles, likewise the periodic apparitions of Mary and some of the saints to the faithful over the centuries? Here one can only conjecture that the risen body of Jesus, Mary, and the saints can rematerialize so as to be perceptible once again to our human senses even though they are in fact continually present to us, though unnoticed as a result of their sharing in the divine life. Our human senses, after all, are known to be severely limited in terms of our range of visual, auditory, and tactile stimuli. There is much more around us than we can directly perceive; even our domestic pets have better sense faculties than we do.

9. See John Polkinghorne, *The God of Hope and the End of the World* (New Haven, CT: Yale University Press, 2002), 140–41: "The writings of the systematic theologians seldom seem to reflect the expectation that cosmic history will continue for many billions of years and that, before its foreseeable end, humanity and all forms of carbon-based life will have vanished from the universe."

10. Kathryn Tanner, "Eschatology without a Future?" in *The End of the World and the Ends of God*, ed. Polkinghorne and Welker, 224.

11. Ibid., 225.

12. Ibid.
13. Polkinghorne, *The God of Hope and the End of the World*, 122–23.
14. Ibid., 123.

CHAPTER 10

1. See, e.g., Stephen G. Post, *Unlimited Love: Altruism, Compassion, and Service* (Philadelphia: Templeton Foundation Press, 2003), vii–xii, 159–202; also Stephen G. Post, Lynn G. Underwood, Jeffrey P. Schloss, and William B. Hurlbut, eds., *Altruism and Altruistic Love: Science, Philosophy, and Religion in Dialogue* (New York: Oxford University Press, 2002), 3–16, 379–86.
2. Pierre Teilhard de Chardin, *The Human Phenomenon*, trans. Sarah Appleton-Weber (Portland, OR: Sussex Academic Press, 1999), 188–91. See also Charles Sanders Peirce, "Evolutionary Love," in *Philosophical Writings of Peirce*, ed. Justus Buchler (New York: Dover Publ., 1955), 361–74; plus Buchler's introduction (xiii–xiv).
3. Pitirim A. Sorokin, *The Ways and Power of Love: Types, Factors, and Techniques of Moral Transformation* (Philadelphia: Templeton Foundation Press, 2002).
4. Ibid., xii.
5. Ibid., 3–14.
6. Ibid., 15–35.
7. Post, *Unlimited Love*, 28–31.
8. Edward O. Wilson, *On Human Nature* (Cambridge, MA: Harvard University Press, 1978), ix. See also by the same author *Sociobiology: The New Synthesis* (Cambridge, MA: Harvard University Press, 1975).
9. Wilson, *Sociobiology*, 3.
10. Richard Dawkins, *The Selfish Gene* (New York: Oxford University Press, 1989), 2.
11. Wilson, *Sociobiology*, 3–4.
12. Ibid., 120–21.
13. Wilson, *On Human Nature*, 153–54.
14. Ibid., 167.
15. Ibid., 3.
16. Michael Ruse, *Can a Darwinian Be a Christian? The Relationship between Science and Religion* (New York: Cambridge University Press, 2001), 126.
17. Ibid., 127.
18. Michael Ruse, "A Darwinian Naturalist's Perspective on Altruism," in *Altruism and Altruistic Love: Science, Philosophy, and Religion in Dialogue*, ed. Stephen Post, Lynn G. Underwood, Jeffrey B. Schloss, and William B. Hurlbut (New York: Oxford University Press, 2002), 164.

19. See Stephen J. Pope, *The Evolution of Altruism and the Ordering of Love* (Washington, DC: Georgetown University Press, 1994); likewise, Aquinas, *Summa Theologiae*, 1a-2ae, q.26.
20. Pope, *The Evolution of Altruism*, 66.
21. Ibid., 140. See also Dawkins, *The Selfish Gene*, v.
22. Pope, *The Evolution of Altruism*, 55.
23. See above, n. 18.
24. Pope, *The Evolution of Altruism*, 137-51.
25. Ibid., 152-60, where he concedes the limited scope of his research and concludes that much more work needs to be done to set in place a Christian understanding of "the ordering of love." Among those additional factors to be considered he proposes careful study of the philosophy of Aristotle and Aquinas—above all, Aquinas's ethical theory. While not denying this, I would rather emphasize the development of a genuine metaphysics of intersubjectivity along the lines sketched in this book. Only with considerable difficulty can one reconceive the philosophy of Aristotle and Aquinas as an implicit metaphysics of intersubjectivity.
26. See Wilson, *Sociobiology*, 397-437.

Chapter 11

1. *Dictionary of Biblical Theology*, ed. Xavier Leon-Dufour, S.J., trans. P. Joseph Cahill, S.J., et al. (New York: Desclee, 1967), 200-201.
2. John G. Stackhouse Jr., *Can God Be Trusted? Faith and the Challenge of Evil* (New York: Oxford University Press, 1988), 104.
3. *The Spiritual Exercises of Saint Ignatius*, trans. George E. Ganss, S.J. (Chicago: Loyola University Press, 1992), 32n.23.
4. Ibid., 42n.53.
5. Ibid., 55n.98, 67n.147, 73n.167.
6. Ibid., 95n.234.

Index

Abelard, Peter, 29
actual entities, 14, 148n7. *See also* actual occasion
actual occasion, xix, 14-18, 24-25, 30-31, 55-58, 70-71, 73-74, 101, 105-08, 110-11, 114, 142n8, 148n7
Ahlgren, Gillian, 147n17
altruism, 116-26
Anselm of Canterbury, 28
Aquinas, Thomas, xvi-xvii, 4-5, 8, 82, 84-86, 98, 121-23, 146n8, 150n25
Aristotle, xvii, 83, 121, 150n25
atomism, 104-06
Augustine, 28, 78, 146n8

baptism, 59-60, 91-93
Barbour, Ian, 141n6, 142n15, 143n2
body, 5-6, 8, 10, 16-18, 60, 98-102, 105, 110-12, 147n20
Bonaventure, 98
Buber, Martin, 9
Buddhism, 61-62
church, 41, 48-50, 53-64, 90-94, 95-96, 144nn6-7
collective power of evil, 41-52, 57, 61, 63-64, 92-94, 96, 116, 138
collective power of good, 41-52, 57, 61, 63-64, 89-102, 116, 138

common element of form, 58-59, 71, 106
common space, 9, 55-56, 107-08
community of interpretation, 68-69, 73
community, 8-12, 41-44, 46-48, 50, 55-60, 63-64, 66-71, 73-74, 89-102, 116, 144nn6-7
Confucianism, 62
consciousness, 15-16, 30, 32, 88, 135
consensus approach to truth, 75-76
consubstantiation, 97, 101, 147n21 *See also* Eucharist
conversion, 29, 129-30
Cooke, Bernard, 91-94, 98-99
cosmic community, xviii, 8-11, 113-15, 138
cosmology, 103, 112
creation, 4-6, 28-29, 55-56, 81-85, 92, 98, 100, 102, 107-08, 110-15, 122-23
creation out of nothing, xvii, 6
creativity, 14-27, 51, 62
  God as creature of creativity, 14, 18-19, 22
crucifixion of Jesus, 32, 37-39, 48, 100, 139

Darwin, Charles, ix, 123
Darwinian, 119-21, 123
Dawkins, Richard, 119-20